Biopharma in China

Sven Agten · Ben Wu

Biopharma in China

Innovation, Trends and Dealmaking

Sven Agten
Pudong, Shanghai, China

Ben Wu
North Point, Hong Kong

ISBN 978-981-97-1470-4   ISBN 978-981-97-1471-1 (eBook)
https://doi.org/10.1007/978-981-97-1471-1

© The Author(s), under exclusive license to Springer Nature Singapore Pte Ltd. 2024

This work is subject to copyright. All rights are solely and exclusively licensed by the Publisher, whether the whole or part of the material is concerned, specifically the rights of translation, reprinting, reuse of illustrations, recitation, broadcasting, reproduction on microfilms or in any other physical way, and transmission or information storage and retrieval, electronic adaptation, computer software, or by similar or dissimilar methodology now known or hereafter developed.

The use of general descriptive names, registered names, trademarks, service marks, etc. in this publication does not imply, even in the absence of a specific statement, that such names are exempt from the relevant protective laws and regulations and therefore free for general use.

The publisher, the authors, and the editors are safe to assume that the advice and information in this book are believed to be true and accurate at the date of publication. Neither the publisher nor the authors or the editors give a warranty, expressed or implied, with respect to the material contained herein or for any errors or omissions that may have been made. The publisher remains neutral with regard to jurisdictional claims in published maps and institutional affiliations.

Cover illustration: © Melisa Hasan

This Palgrave Macmillan imprint is published by the registered company Springer Nature Singapore Pte Ltd.
The registered company address is: 152 Beach Road, #21-01/04 Gateway East, Singapore 189721, Singapore

Paper in this product is recyclable.

Introduction

China is not only the second biggest economy in the world, it's also one of the most dynamic markets, especially the healthcare sector which only during the last decade started to grow exponentially. A variety of factors, including extended life expectancy, an aging population and greater expectations about quality of life have driven China's healthcare market to become the second-largest in the world. There has been significant investment in local healthcare infrastructure, market reforms and support for innovation through the 'Healthy China 2030' initiative, which was announced in 2016. One particular beneficiary of this evolution within the healthcare sector, are the Chinese biopharma companies. A decade ago the Chinese biopharma sector was as good as non-existent. The Chinese pharmaceutical market consisted almost entirely of generic medicines, while innovative medicines needed to be imported from abroad. Now however Chinese companies are out-licensing homegrown innovative drugs, something that few could have predicted only a few years ago. Then the China biopharma innovation ecosystem was barely emerging, and it was taking a lot of foresight to envision what could come next.

This book takes a deep dive into the evolution and growth of the Chinese biopharma sector, from its humble beginnings till what the sector has become now, a key part of the global biopharma market. It also encompasses the first boom and bust cycle of the sector and focuses on the drivers and challenges of the biopharma sector in China. The book provides an overview of its current state, highlighting key advancements, milestones and the future of the industry. It also shows how Chinese biopharma evolved, and how Chinese biopharma companies had a unique development trajectory, vastly different than its counterparts in the US, Europe or Japan. We show how Chinese biotechs transformed themselves from fast followers to innovators, and how they excel in 'innovation on innovation'. The book also gives insights into the world of Chinese healthcare venture capitalists, in what kind of biopharma companies they invest, and how they created a massive investment bubble, which started to burst from 2021 on. The latter left the sector in disarray, resulting in investors and companies alike to look for new strategies to survive and thrive further.

Furthermore, we also show how foreign companies need to deal with the Chinese biopharma market and its companies, what works and what does not. China cannot only be treated anymore as a market, but increasingly needs to be seen as a source of innovation. In addition, the book also provides practical advice for foreign companies which want to raise funds from Chinese investors or strike a partnership with Chinese companies.

The insights the book provides are based on the experiences of the authors. Both have an insider's perspective as they had front row seats to the growth of the Chinese biopharma sector. Ben Wu has an extensive career in the pharma sector, was involved in several Chinese biotechs, and founding CEO of a China originated biopharma, Citrine Medicine. As such he lived through the boom years of the Chinese biopharma sector. He engaged in fundraising, licensing deals and all other operational aspects of running a biopharma in China. Sven Agten is an experienced businessman and executive, lives and works in Shanghai, and is a keen observer of trends and opportunities in China. He lives nearby one of the biggest biotech parks in China, the Zhangjiang High-Tech Park. Many of his friends and neighbors are active in the biopharma sector. As such Sven witnessed over the years first-hand the evolution of the biopharma sector in China. Both have a unique view of one of the new drivers of growth of the Chinese economy, and experienced first-hand how China transformed itself from a maker of generic medicine to an inventor of innovative medicines.

Contents

The Chinese Healthcare and Pharmaceutical Market:
Ignore at Your Own Peril — 1

China Regulatory and Legal Reforms: Gateway
to Innovation and Global Integration — 21

The Golden Age of Chinese Biopharma Sector,
2014–2021: Explosive Growth in a Thriving Ecosystem — 41

Innovation in the Chinese Biopharma Sector: From
Me-too to First-in-Class — 71

The Art of the Biopharma Deal: The China Angle — 101

End of the First Cycle, 2022 and Beyond: A Drastic Reset,
Increased Challenges But Also New Opportunities — 113

Afterword — 143

Index — 147

The Chinese Healthcare and Pharmaceutical Market: Ignore at Your Own Peril

Abstract China's healthcare industry is one of the largest sectors of GDP for the country. The Chinese healthcare market is the second biggest globally. The surge in demand for superior healthcare and services is driving swift growth across various healthcare segments. Factors like an aging population, a major disease burden and increased spending power, resulted in a substantial increase in spending on healthcare. The government also has recognized this growing healthcare needs of the population and prioritized the increased importance of providing better quality and more accessible healthcare to its citizens. China realized that it must provide better medicines, technology and services to its people. To address all these issues, in 2016 the 'Healthy China 2030' initiative was launched. The aim is also to increase the local and global market share in medicines and medical technology products, promote made-in-China manufacturing and create a few global healthcare industrial champions. As a result of that China has grown into a major pharmaceutical player, home of 4,500 pharmaceutical companies, a top producer of Active Pharmaceutical Ingredients (APIs), generic medicines and of course Traditional Chinese Medicine (TCM). The newest addition is the biopharma sector and its focus on innovative medicines. Innovative drug discovery is only a decade old in China, but the sector a seen an explosive growth, combined with massive investments from foreign and domestic healthcare investors.

Keywords Active Pharmaceutical Ingredient (API) · Drug manufacturing · Generic medicines · Healthy China 2030 · Healthcare market · Innovative drugs · Medical insurance · Patented medicines · Pharmaceutical companies · Pharmaceutical market

In most countries around the world, healthcare is one of the most thriving and lucrative sectors of the economy. China is no different. With high levels of growth due to an increase in household incomes, China's healthcare industry is one of the largest sectors of GDP in the country. The surge in demand for superior healthcare and services is driving swift growth across various healthcare segments. Factors like an aging population, a major disease burden and increased spending power, resulted in a substantial increase in spending on healthcare. The government also has recognized this growing healthcare needs of the population and prioritized the increased importance of providing better quality and more accessible healthcare to its citizens. China realized that it must provide better medicines, technology and services to its people. To address all these issues, in 2016 the 'Healthy China 2030' initiative was launched. It sets out the framework and targets for domestic healthcare companies, and the healthcare sector as a whole. The main goal is that very clear parameters and indicators should reach the level of high-income countries. The aim is also to increase the local and global market share in medicines and medical technology products, promote made-in-China manufacturing and create a few global healthcare industrial champions. Basically 'Healthy China 2030' is the guide for all reforms and programs.[1]

China indeed has a clear ambition to improve the healthcare outcomes for its 1.4 billion people. These include achieving an average life expectancy of 79+, eliminating major diseases, improving drug safety, the

---

[1] Melchers. 2022. Healthy China 2030—Recent trends and developments. www.melchers-china.com/posts/healthy-china-2030-recent-trends-and-developments. Accessed on November 2, 2023.

provision of world-leading health technology and establishing an innovative health industry that is a pillar of the economy. An expanding universal health insurance scheme that covers an aging population across rural and urban areas underlies this ambition.[2] Over the last two decades China invested heavily in all this. As a result, China's healthcare industry has seen rapid growth over the past decade and comprised of approximately 6.7% of the GDP in 2021, with a 50% increase targeted by 2030.[3] In 2021, total revenue for the healthcare market was estimated to be around US$1.2 trillion), making it the second biggest healthcare market in the world.[4] Healthcare spending in China between 2010 and 2018 grew faster than GDP. Today only the US' healthcare market is bigger with an estimated size of US$4.3 trillion.[5]

CHINA HAS GROWN INTO A MAJOR PHARMACEUTICAL PLAYER

An essential part of any healthcare market is its pharmaceutical sector. China's pharma industry has come a long way. For a long time after the foundation of the PRC in 1949, China faced the challenges of drug shortages. Because of a historical lack of an industrial basis, China

---

[2] Lexology. 2023. China's healthcare industry is booming: What investment opportunities does it bring? www.lexology.com/library/detail.aspx?g=ab062882-78bc-46e6-92ad-9cc92d83d0f7. Accessed on November 2, 2023.

[3] Moore MS Advisory. 2023. Industry Insights: China's evolving healthcare sector. https://www.msadvisory.com/china-healthcare-industry/#:~:text=China's%20healthcare%20industry%20has%20seen,hygiene%20by%20the%20Chinese%20government. Accessed on November 25, 2023.

[4] China Briefing. 2023. Understanding China's rapidly growing healthcare market. https://www.china-briefing.com/news/understanding-chinas-rapidly-growing-healthcare-market/. Accessed on November 24, 2023.

[5] Centers for Medicare & Medicaid Services. 2023. Historical. www.cms.gov/data-research/statistics-trends-and-reports/national-health-expenditure-data/historical#:~:text=U.S.%20health%20care%20spending%20grew,For%20additional%20information%2C%20see%20below. Accessed on November 24, 2023.

could not even produce the most basic drugs. The domestic pharmaceutical industry was set up with the help of the Soviets but experienced a long-term stagnation and modest improvement in its manufacturing capacity. In the 1990s after the opening up of China, the industry began to upgrade its manufacturing capabilities through multiple channels, including experimenting joint ventures with foreign pharma companies, direct procurement of manufacturing equipment and techniques from Western countries, and encouraging private investment into drug manufacturing, and so forth.[6] Consequently, in the recent decades China has become a major pharmaceutical player. China is now a country long known for producing generics and raw materials. It has a huge manufacturing industry for raw materials and generics, and a rapidly emerging biopharma sector. Since joining the World Trade Organization in 2001, China's pharmaceutical industry has experienced remarkable growth. In 2021, it accounted for 12% of the global pharmaceutical market, second only to the United States, which accounted for a substantial 40% of the world's total revenue.[7] The pharmaceutical market in China grew from US$200 billion in 2016, to US$271 billion in 2022. According to Deloitte It is projected to grow to a size of US$332 billion in 2025.[8] By comparison, the US pharmaceutical market was worth US$567 billion in 2022.[9]

---

[6] National Library of Medicine. 2023. Success and challenges of China's healthcare reform: A four-decade perspective spanning 1985–2023. https://www.ncbi.nlm.nih.gov/pmc/articles/PMC10469830/. Accessed on November 24, 2023.

[7] Statista. 2023. Share of pharmaceutical value worldwide 2021, by country. www.statista.com/statistics/1246593/value-share-of-pharmaceutical-companies-worldwide-by-country/. Accessed on November 24, 2023.

[8] Deloitte. 2023. Navigating China's pharmaceutical industry landscape. https://www.pwc.com/us/en/industries/pharma-life-sciences/china-pharmaceutical-strategy.html. Accessed on November 23, 2023.

[9] Insights 10. 2023. US Pharmaceutical market analysis. https://www.insights10.com/report/us-pharmaceutical-market-analysis/. Accessed on November 23, 2023.

China pharmaceutical market size in USD Bn (2016-2022)

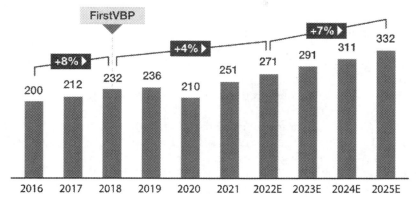

Source Deloitte. 2023. Navigating China's pharmaceutical industry landscape

Active Pharmaceutical Ingredients (API)

As production shifted from West to East, many Western companies outsourced production. China is now the top producer of Active Pharmaceutical Ingredients or APIs. An API is a component of a drug that impacts health, for instance suppressing a disease or a symptom. A simple API is a raw material that is included in medicines. It is a biologically active component used in drugs (capsules, tablets, injectables, etc.) to produce the intended outcome.[10] Very few companies manage and control the whole process from raw material to finished drug. There used to be a time when pharmaceutical companies managed everything of the production end-to-end, but now they prefer to outsource APIs. Until the mid-1990s, the West and Japan produced 90% of the world's APIs. But

---

[10] Beroe. 2023. API Pharmaceutical: What is API in pharma, difference between API & Formulation. https://www.beroeinc.com/blogs/api-in-pharma/. Accessed on November 23, 2023.

in 2017 it was estimated that China alone was producing about 40% of all APIs. China accounts for more than 60% of vitamin B1 and 40% of aspirins exported globally. The country has an advantage in low-cost and off-patent APIs. And even India, another pharmaceutical giant, depends heavily on China. India accounts for about 20% of global generic drug demand by volume, but it imports about 70% of the APIs from China. A drug generally can be produced 20% less expensive in China than in India, largely thanks to access to cheaper raw materials, which can be up to two-thirds of the total production costs. China also has a production scale advantage.[11]

The Chinese government itself has clearly understood the value of the API industry. Since the 2000s the government has implemented numerous laws and regulations that have encouraged API production. Western companies were also very open to offload the API production, as it's a rather dirty and very polluting business.[12] This all means that China simply plays an indispensable role in the supply chain of many APIs. It is exactly this dominance that Western countries now try to overturn as the Covid-pandemic and geopolitical tensions expose this supply chain vulnerability. The zero-tolerance approach in China and the numerous lockdowns caused significant shipping delays, which led to shortages in Europe and the US of standardly used medicines.[13]

Generics, Patented Pharmaceuticals and OTC

The Chinese pharmaceutical market is divided into three segments: generics, patented pharmaceuticals and over the counter (OTC) drugs. The most expensive and most innovative drugs are the patented pharmaceuticals, developed by biopharma companies at very high costs. When a medicine is first developed, the pharmaceutical company that discovers and markets it, receives a patent on its new drug. The patent usually lasts

---

[11] Nikkei Assia. 2022. The great medicine migration. https://asia.nikkei.com/static/vdata/infographics/chinavaccine-3/. Accessed on November 23, 2023.

[12] Nikkei Assia. 2022. The great medicine migration. https://asia.nikkei.com/static/vdata/infographics/chinavaccine-3/. Accessed on November 23, 2023.

[13] Forbes. 2022. The Covid-19 pandemic highlights intensified drug advantages. https://www.forbes.com/sites/forbestechcouncil/2022/07/14/the-covid-19-pandemic-highlights-intensified-drug-shortages/?sh=66d34ba78554. Accessed on November 23, 2023.

for 20 years, to give the innovator a chance to recoup its research investment. After the patent expires, a generic version of the drug may become available.[14] A generic drug is then a medication created to be the same as an already marketed brand-name drug in dosage form, safety, strength, route of administration, quality, performance characteristics and intended use. This means that generic medicines work in the same way and provide the same clinical benefit as the brand-name medicines. But they are much cheaper. In the US for instance generics account for 90% of prescriptions, but only 22% of the total drug costs.[15] As a result, generic drugs have emerged rapidly as a crucial means for many countries to reduce national healthcare expenses. OTC drugs are nonprescription medicines. They refer to medicine that you can buy without a prescription. In China, Traditional Chinese Medicine (TCM) is generally used and preferred above Western medicine. These treatments and supplements are generally over-the-counter type medicine, similar to how Western grocery stores might carry cough syrup or medicated ointment.

China has been a traditionally generic drug market. Due to the low purchasing power and a robust local manufacturing sector, Chinese drug makers focused on producing generic drugs, once the global patents on these medicines expired. In 2016 it was reported that of about 170,000 drug approvals in China, over 95% are generics.[16] Before 2010, the top 20 China healthcare companies were mostly generic drug makers.[17] That also meant that until a few years ago, most new drugs in China came from abroad.

---

[14] Association of Accessible Medicines. 2020. https://accessiblemeds.org/generic-medicines. Accessed on November 23, 2023.

[15] Association of Accessible Medicines. 2020. https://accessiblemeds.org/generic-medicines. Accessed on November 23, 2023.

[16] FiercePharma. 2018. China pushes generics over brands with another round of new pharma policies. https://www.fiercepharma.com/pharma-asia/china-pushes-another-round-policy-favors-generic-drugs. Accessed on November 23, 2023.

[17] Invesco. 2021. What's driving growth in China's biotech industry? www.invesco.com/apac/en/institutional/insights/china/whats-driving-growth-in-chinas-biotech-industry.html#src4. Accessed on November 23, 2023.

The generic medicine market in China is however undergoing a gradual reform. The government started to eliminate a significant number of substandard generic drugs, while at the same from 2017 onwards it implemented new price reduction policies. This led to reduced margins for drug makers. At the same time due to regulatory reforms, a rapidly aging population and affluent middle class that is willing to spend on quality healthcare products and services as outlined, there were growing opportunities in the biotech sector. Consequently, generic drug makers in the country have been pushed to innovate and move up the value chain. Large Chinese pharma companies are now spending more on R&D and specifically are looking to innovative areas such as oncology drugs. At the same time biotech companies in China have mushroomed and are all focusing on the development of innovative drugs. Since a decade now the market has seen a robust growth in biological pharmaceuticals, or biologics, which are much more difficult to produce than ordinary drugs, as it requires biotechnology. Biotech drugs are favorable as compared to chemical drugs as they have fewer side effects.[18] These biologics differ from traditional drugs in terms of material sources, structural complexities, manufacturing process and regulatory requirements. As a result, biologics have a higher development price too.

China's pharma sector is shifting away from a manufacturing hub, and gradually becoming a key R&D player. From 2010–2020 more biological drug companies emerged in the top 20 Chinese healthcare companies.[19] In 2020 the size of the Chinese biopharma market was US$47.6 billion and is projected to grow to US$111 billion in 2025.[20] Despite the growth of the market, the Chinese biopharma market is still in its infancy. Sales of biologics still lag behind compared to other markets. In 2019 for example, sales of the top ten biotech drugs (biologics) globally were in the range of US$ six to 20 billion, while Chinese biologic sales were in

---

[18] Invesco. 2021. What's driving growth in China's biotech industry? www.invesco.com/apac/en/institutional/insights/china/whats-driving-growth-in-chinas-biotech-industry.html#src4. Accessed on November 23, 2023.

[19] Invesco. 2021. What's driving growth in China's biotech industry? www.invesco.com/apac/en/institutional/insights/china/whats-driving-growth-in-chinas-biotech-industry.html#src4. Accessed on November 23, 2023.

[20] China Briefing. 2022. China's biopharma industry. Market prospects, investment paths. https://www.china-briefing.com/news/china-booming-biopharmaceuticals-market-innovation-investment-opportunities/. Accessed on November 24, 2023.

the range of RMB three to five billion, or US$460 to 750 million. In 2021 biotech-driven treatments accounted for only 12% of the China's total drug market.[21]

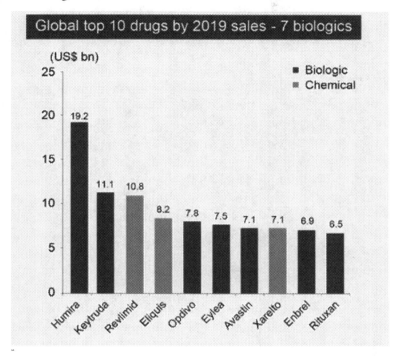

Source Invesco. 2021. What's driving growth in China's biotech industry?

[21] Invesco. 2021. What's driving growth in China's biotech industry? www.invesco.com/apac/en/institutional/insights/china/whats-driving-growth-in-chinas-biotech-industry.html#src4. Accessed on November 23, 2023.

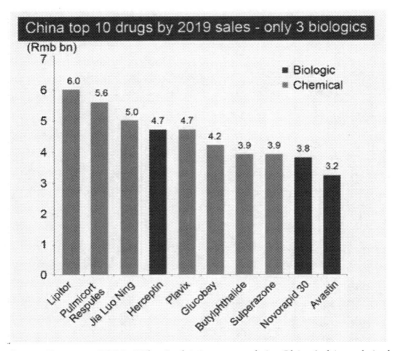

Source Invesco. 2021. What's driving growth in China's biotech industry?

According to a consumer market insights report by Statista, China generates the most over-the-counter revenue, accounting for US$29.36 billion of the US$145.3 billion in global revenue. Digestive and metabolic drugs and systemic anti-infective drugs account for 14% of the Chinese pharmaceutical market. Cardiovascular and central nervous system drugs each account for slightly less at 13% each.[22]

PHARMACEUTICAL AND BIOPHARMA COMPANIES

There are 4,500 pharmaceutical manufacturers in China, led by a small number of big players. The market is still very fragmented, but experts believe the industry will see increased competition and consolidation

[22] Pharmanews Intelligence. 2023. Comparing global pharmaceutical markets: US, UK and China. https://pharmanewsintel.com/features/comparing-global-pharmaceutical-markets-the-us-uk-and-china. Accessed on November 25, 2023.

in the coming years, driven partly by regulatory reforms. In 2022, Sinopharm Group, Shanghai Pharmaceuticals, and Jointown Pharmaceutical Group were the top three Chinese pharmaceutical companies.[23] Other well-known names are Hengrui, Jumpcan Pharmaceuticals, Fosun Pharma, Grand Pharma Holding, Meheco, SCPC Pharmaceutical and so forth. The biggest bulk of the domestic companies are still focused on the domestic market, still generating most of the sales from generic medicines or TCM but trying to increase the scale of their operations and transform their innovative capabilities. Besides the top players, most of the other pharmaceutical companies have not developed any patented drugs.[24] But many of them will eventually need to focus on the development and sales of innovative drugs too. Plagued with scandals of low quality and ineffective products considered obsolete elsewhere, questionable operators and poor supply chains, both the government and the public have pushed for the sector to be cleaned up. Over the last decade the policy response has been to significantly raise the bar on generic drug quality, encourage local companies to innovate premium drugs and expand access to better medicines.

Foreign multinationals traditionally occupied the space of innovative medicines in China. For Novartis, Eli Lily, Roche, Sanofi and MSD the Chinese market accounts for 5–10% of their global sales. For AstraZeneca this is even 16%.

[23] Pharmanews Intelligence. 2023. Comparing global pharmaceutical markets: US, UK and China. https://pharmanewsintel.com/features/comparing-global-pharmaceutical-markets-the-us-uk-and-china. Accessed on November 25, 2023.

[24] China Project. 2022. China's pharma companies are spending big on R&D, but global success remains elusive. https://thechinaproject.com/2022/05/09/chinas-pharma-companies-are-spending-big-on-rd-but-global-success-remains-elusive/. Accessed on November 15, 2022.

Company	Total Sales/US$ billion	YoY Growth	Sales in China/US$ billion	YoY Growth	Proportion of Sales in China to Total Sales
AstraZeneca[1]	37.42	38%	5.99	12%	16%
MSD[2]	48.70	17%	4.26	60%	9%
Roche[3]	69.01	9%	3.6	4%	5%
Sanofi[4]	44.55	7%	3.21	7.9%	7%
Novartis[5]	51.62	6%	3.05	18%	6%
Lilly[6]	28.31	15%	1.66	49%	6%
J & J[7]	93.77	14%	/	/	/
Pfizer[8]	81.3	95%	/	/	/
Abbvie[9]	56.19	23%	/	/	/
GSK[10]	46.91	5%	/	/	/
BMS[11]	46.38	9%	/	/	/

Source Baipharm. 2022. Multinational pharma companies record sales growth in 2021

A new breed of companies is the Chinese biotechs. Innovative biopharma in China is basically just ten years old, but it witnessed an explosive growth, nurtured by a combination of factors.

With the largest population in the world, China provides not just huge commercial opportunities, but also a massive set of potential patients to enroll into clinical trials. China's National Medical Products Administration (NMPA) has streamlined the clinical trial and drug approval process, including priority and special reviews as well as breakthrough therapy designations for innovative products that target unmet medical needs in China. The National Reimbursement Drug List is being updated more frequently and prioritizes the entry of newly approved novel drugs. Lastly, rule changes allowed pre-revenue/pre-profit biotech companies to be listed in the Hong Kong Stock Exchange (HKEX) or Shanghai Stock Exchange's Science and Technology Innovative Board (STAR). Combined together, all of these factors can be seen as a rocket propeller for growth. Today China is home to a vibrant biopharma sector with thousands of biotech companies. There are vastly different than the traditional Chinese pharmaceutical companies, as these biotechs focused immediately on the development of innovative medicines. Most of them were set up by Chinese scientists and Sr. executives from foreign multinationals who often spent decades abroad and had as such experience with drug development and manufacturing. Meteoric rises in valuation and global visibility of some of the leaders like Wuxi AppTec, Beigene or Innovent Biologics have inspired many others to follow this path.

HEALTHCARE FACILITIES AND SERVICES

China has a dual healthcare system. There is free public healthcare available to almost all citizens. There are also specialty and private hospitals. These are generally used by those who have private insurance or who can afford it. Because of this, they usually offer a higher standard of care, specialty medicine and more specialized areas of practice, such as cosmetic surgery. At the end of 2021, there were over one million healthcare institutions in China. Among these, there were 36,570 hospitals, of which 11,804 were public and 24,766 were private. This means there was an average of two hospitals for every 100,000 residents. This number was expected to increase to three for every 100,000 residents in 2022 and 2023. Revenue from hospitals reached US$580 billion in 2021. In the same year people visited hospitals and medical institutions an average of six times, mostly at public hospitals. There was a total of 3.27 billion visits to public hospitals that year and 610 million visits to private hospitals.[25] Public hospitals currently provide about 85% of medical care in China. While public hospitals focus mostly on general medical care, private hospitals usually offer more specialist medical services like ophthalmology and stomatology.[26] Hospitals in China are organized according to a three-tier system that recognizes a hospital's ability to provide medical care, provide medical education and conduct medical research. Based on this, hospitals are designated as primary, secondary, or tertiary institutions. The top hospitals are located in the big cities. Because of this there is a very uneven distribution. Most of the top 100 hospitals in northern China are

---

[25] China Briefing. 2023. Understanding China's rapidly growing healthcare market. https://www.china-briefing.com/news/understanding-chinas-rapidly-growing-healthcare-market/. Accessed on November 19, 2023.

[26] The China Project. 2022. Why China's hospitals are going out of business in the middle of a pandemic. https://thechinaproject.com/2022/12/06/why-chinas-hospitals-are-going-out-of-business-in-the-middle-of-a-pandemic/. Accessed on November 19, 2023.

concentrated in Beijing. Although the economy in South China is relatively developed, medical resources are mainly concentrated in Shanghai, Changsha, Wuhan and Guangzhou.[27]

Source China Briefing. 2023. Understanding China's rapidly growing healthcare market

In 2021, there were almost 14 million people working in the healthcare industry. Of these, 60.6% were working in hospitals, 31.7% were working in primary healthcare facilities, village clinics, outpatient departments and so on. 6.9% were working in specialized public healthcare institutions. Among the healthcare professionals, there are 4.3 million doctors (including assistant doctors) and just over five million registered nurses. This means that in 2021 there were around 3.04 doctors and 3.56 nurses for every 1,000 people.[28]

---

[27] National Library of Medicine. 2023. Achievements and challenges of the healthcare system in China. https://www.ncbi.nlm.nih.gov/pmc/articles/PMC10292030/#:~:text=Hospitals%20in%20China%20are%20organized,%2C%20secondary%2C%20or%20tertiary%20institutions. Accessed on November 19, 2023.

[28] China Briefing. 2023. Understanding China's rapidly growing healthcare market. https://www.china-briefing.com/news/understanding-chinas-rapidly-growing-healthcare-market/. Accessed on November 19, 2023.

One of the big problems in China is primary care. Many people who seek medical help often bypass general practitioners and go straight to hospital-based specialists. As a result, visiting a hospital doctor can still be a complicated business with lots of paperwork and lengthy queues before and after consultations. Queues in Chinese hospitals are legendary. People need to stand in line to pay fees for registration, testing and treatment. It was quite common that patients in China used to have to set aside at least half a day for visiting a hospital doctor. At the same time visiting a doctor was deemed to be expensive. So many Chinese faced the issue that it was difficult and expensive to see a doctor. To partly solve this problem, there has been a rapid expansion of the general practitioner (GP) workforce in China in recent years. The number of GPs per 10,000 residents has nearly doubled from 1.38 in 2015 to 2.61 in 2019, with them to increase the number of GPs to five per 10,000 residents by 2030.[29]

CHALLENGES AND OPPORTUNITIES

The availability of healthcare resources in China has improved significantly over the last two decades. China has long had shortages of key resources, such as medical professionals, institutions and pharmaceuticals. Today, however—at least in urban regions—these have largely caught up with international levels. That being said, there are still significant challenges which at the same time are driving forces behind the future growth of the pharmaceutical sector.

China's demographic structure has been changing in recent years. Increasing life expectancy and the consequences of the one-child policy led to a rapid aging of society and a slow decline in population growth. The 2021 census data revealed that overall, the average age in China is 38.8 years old. 264 million people, representing 18.7% of the population are 60 years or older.[30] That means that sooner rather than later the number of retirees outpaces the number of young people entering

[29] BMC. 2022. Recruitment of general practitioners in China: A scoping review of strategies and challenges. https://bmcprimcare.biomedcentral.com/articles/10.1186/s12875-022-01854-0#:~:text=There%20has%20been%20a%20rapid,2019%20%5B1%2C%202%5D. Accessed on November 19, 2023.

[30] China Briefing. 2021. China's census 2021: 5 takeaways for foreign investors. https://www.china-briefing.com/news/chinas-census-2021-5-takeaways-for-foreign-investors/. Accessed on September 8, 2023.

the workforce. According to the United Nations, by 2035, 400 million people, or 30% of the population, will be 60 or older.[31] The rising share of elderly people in China's population has far-reaching implications for Chinese society and will be an underlying driver for the growth of China's healthcare market. Elderly citizens, with extended life expectancy, will require social support and healthcare coverage for longer, placing more pressure on the healthcare industry and driving demand for services.

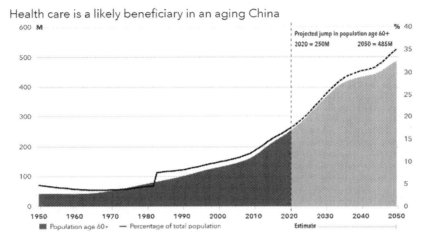

Health care is a likely beneficiary in an aging China

Source United Nations, Department of Economic and Social Affairs. Population Division. 2019

Besides an aging population, China also faces a major disease burden. Higher incomes mean changes in lifestyle, less healthy eating habits and increased consumption. This results to an increase in lifestyle diseases such as diabetes, high blood pressure and obesity. China has one of the highest proportions worldwide of overweight and obesity among children under five. About 8.3% or roughly 5 million children were overweight or obese in 2020, and the numbers are still rising. Cardiovascular diseases affect more than 300 million people and is the leading cause of death,

---

[31] CNN, 2023. Chinese cities are so broke, they're cutting medical benefits for seniors. https://edition.cnn.com/2023/03/31/economy/china-pension-protests-aging-society-intl-hnk/index.html. Accessed on September 8, 2023.

accounting for 40% of mortality in China. Between 1990 and 2015, case rates of cardiovascular diseases almost doubled in China.[32]

Lung cancer is a serious problem in China. The country is the largest producer and consumer of tobacco in the world. There are more than 300 million smokers in China, nearly one-third of the world's total. In addition, over 700 million non-smokers in China, including about 180 million children, are exposed to second-hand smoke (SHS) at least once a day in a typical week.[33] Due to smoking and air pollution unsurprisingly China has a disproportionally high amount of lung cancer cases. With estimates of about 2,206,771 new cases and 1,796,144 deaths globally in 2020, China accounted for about 37% of all newly diagnosed cases and 40% of deaths from lung cancer.[34]

Projected 2030 Global Disease Prevalence
China, Europe and United States

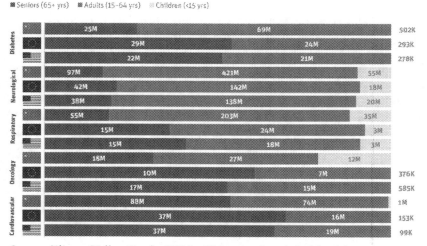

Source Silicon Valley Bank. 2020. China in the global healthcare system

[32] Nature. 2023. By the numbers: China's changing diet. www.nature.com/articles/d41586-023-02060-3. Accessed on November 2, 2023.

[33] World Health Organization. 2023. Tobacco in China. https://www.who.int/china/health-topics/tobacco. Accessed on November 1, 2023.

[34] ScienceDirect. 2022. Lung cancer incidence and mortality in China: Updated statistics and an overview of temporal trends from 2000 to 2016. www.sciencedirect.com/science/article/pii/S2667005422000436. Accessed on November 2, 2023.

China is home now to the largest middle class in the world. The middle class is also very affluent with spending power and looking to spend more money on high-quality healthcare products and services. Over the last years consumer awareness and demand for better healthcare has risen dramatically in China. The Chinese middle class is expected to generate more than one-quarter of all global consumption growth over the next decade, and is thus also demanding more and better medicines, medical equipment and services. The market for medical devices for instance was estimated to be worth US$45 billion in 2023, of which currently two-thirds of all equipment is being imported from abroad.[35] The same goes for the market of innovative medicines. Even before the pandemic vaccine quality was discussed extensively in social media, and vaccines made by multinationals that are available in China are often out of stock because demand exceeds supply.[36] Between 2012 and 2022 annual health expenditure per citizen in China tripled to almost 1,000 US$ per person.[37] There is still a lot of room for China's healthcare expenditure to grow, as it is still below that of many high-income nations. Germany's healthcare expenditure per capita in 2021 was US$7,383, while South Korea's was US$3,914.[38]

Lastly there is an expansion of insurance coverage. The Chinese government has established a healthcare insurance system that covers almost 96% of the population and benefits more than 1.36 billion people. This system includes basic medical insurance conducted by the government. There are differences in coverage. Working urban residents pay the most insurance funds and have the highest reimbursement ratio,

---

[35] Global Data. 2023. Impact of China on medical devices industry—Thematic intelligence. www.globaldata.com/store/report/impact-of-china-on-medical-devices-industry-theme-analysis/. Accessed on November 25, 2023.

[36] Capital Group. 2020. China's biopharma industry moves closer to inflection point. https://www.capitalgroup.com/institutional/insights/articles/china-biopharma-stocks.html. Accessed on November 24, 2023.

[37] Statista. 2023. Health expenditure per Chinese citizen from 2012 to 2022. www.statista.com/statistics/279401/per-capita-health-expenditure-in-china/. Accessed on November 25, 2023.

[38] China Briefing. 2023. Understanding China's rapidly growing healthcare market. https://www.china-briefing.com/news/understanding-chinas-rapidly-growing-healthcare-market/. Accessed on November 19, 2023.

followed by non-working residents and the rural population.[39] Funding of health coverage comes from the central government, local governments, employers, and the participants, and the level of funding varies by geographic area. Medical insurance reimbursement policies vary in different provinces or cities according to the level of economic development. Chinese health insurance plans have narrow restrictions on what is covered, high co-payments and very low coverage maximums.[40] Furthermore, the system is not standardized yet with regional differences, and gasps in reimbursement. Because of these limitations wealthier Chinese citizens opt for a commercial health insurance. These health insurance plans offer more comprehensive coverage with better payout ratios and include more innovative therapies not being reimbursed by basic medical insurance. The premium income of China's health insurance has therefore increased rapidly between 2011 and 2020 with a compound annual growth rate exceeding 30%.[41] In 2022, overall premium income from health insurance in China exceeded US$130 Billion.[42] It is expected that this growth will continue in the future, driving healthcare spending even higher.

[39] National Library of Medicine. 2023. Achievements and challenges of the healthcare system in China. https://www.ncbi.nlm.nih.gov/pmc/articles/PMC10292030/#:~:text=Hospitals%20in%20China%20are%20organized,%2C%20secondary%2C%20or%20tertiary%20institutions. Accessed on November 19, 2023.

[40] The New York Times. 2023. How health insurance works in China and how it's changing. https://www.nytimes.com/2023/02/23/business/china-health-insurance-explained.html. Accessed on November 19, 2023.

[41] MCOL. 2021. China's commercial health insurance market. https://mcolblog.com/kcblog/2021/8/10/chinas-commercial-health-insurance-market-1.html. Accessed on November 19, 2023.

[42] Statista. 2023. Premium revenue from health insurance in China from 2012 to 2022. https://www.statista.com/statistics/1032552/china-premium-revenue-from-health-insurance/#:~:text=In%202022%2C%20overall%20premium%20income,yuan%20in%20the%20previous%20year. Accessed on November 19, 2023.

China Regulatory and Legal Reforms: Gateway to Innovation and Global Integration

Abstract Until a decade ago the Chinese pharma sector lagged behind internationally. Its products were of subpar quality, there was no standardization and innovation was non-existent. The 'Healthy China 2030' initiative however, changed all that. Over the last decade China has made significant strides in upgrading and updating all aspects of the healthcare system. A key pillar in these upgrades were the changes being made in its legal and regulatory framework for the pharmaceutical sector. This was needed in order to integrate with the global pharma market, to get better access to innovative medicines, and pave the way for the development of a real homegrown biopharma industry. The major reforms, initiated in 2015 have significantly improved all aspects of the biopharmaceutical sector. Major hurdles have been removed. By 2023 China had implemented the guidelines of the International Conference on Harmonization of Technical Requirements for Registration of Pharmaceuticals for Human Use (ICH). This is undoubtedly a milestone achievement, as it greatly improves market access for foreign companies, helps Chinese companies to venture outside China and improves patients' access to innovative medicines. At the same the Chinese government has also introduced the Volume Based Procurement (VBP) policy, implemented the National Reimbursement Drug List (NRDL) and the process of price negotiations to get entry on the list. In this way the government wants to keep the price of medicines under control.

Keywords International Conference on Harmonization of Technical Requirements for Registration of Pharmaceuticals for Human Use (ICH) · Marketing Authorization Holder (MAH) · National Healthcare Security Administration (NHSA) · National Medical Products Administration (NMPA) · National Reimbursement Drug List (NRDL) · Patent Law · Price negotiation · Real-world evidence (RWE) · Regulatory framework · Volume Based Procurement (VBP)

Until a decade ago the Chinese pharma sector lagged behind internationally. Its products were of subpar quality, there was no standardization and innovation was non-existent. The 'Healthy China 2030' initiative, however, changed all that. Over the last decade China has made significant strides in upgrading and updating all aspects of the healthcare system. A key pillar in these upgrades were the changes being made in its legal and regulatory framework for the pharmaceutical sector. This was needed in order to integrate with the global pharma market, to get better access to innovative medicines, and to pave the way for the development of a real homegrown biopharma industry.

In order to understand how China has structured everything concerning pharmaceuticals and medicines in general, we need to have a brief look at the responsibilities of the three government agencies involved. First there is the National Medical Products Administration (NMPA) which handles pre-market affairs, such as drugs' market authorization and approval. Secondly there is the National Healthcare Security Administration (NHSA) which focuses on ensuring reasonable pricing for drugs, especially pricings for public purchase. Lastly there is the State Administration for Market Regulation (SAMR) which oversees competition-related issues, such as anticompetitive practices.[1]

---

[1] Lexology. 2023. A general introduction to pharmaceutical IP and competition issues in China. www.lexology.com/library/detail.aspx?g=270ff683-97f3-4af6-992f-ce8cd9f60922&utm_source=lexology+daily+newsfeed&utm_medium=html+email+-+body+-+general+section&utm_campaign=lexology+subscriber+daily+feed&utm_content=lexology+daily+newsfeed+2023-09-19&utm_term=. Accessed on September 20, 2023.

NMPA, NHSA AND SAMR

The NMPA, formerly known as the China Food and Drug Administration or CFDA, is the Chinese agency regulating drugs and medical devices. It handles its affairs mostly pursuant to the Drug Administration Law of the People's Republic of China, originally enacted in 1984, but last amended in 2019 (the Drug Administration Law).[2] The Drug Administration Law includes provisions and regulations on drug research and development, approval procedures,' approval holders obligations, requirements for manufacture and marketing, responsibilities of medical institutions, market supervision, pricing and advertising guidelines, and so on.

The NHSA is the main governing body of, among other things, China's medical insurance schemes, in which employees and employers each contribute a portion of the employee's monthly salary to the employee's medical insurance account. It enforces the Social Security Law of the People's Republic of China and the Basic Medical Care and Health Promotion Law of the People's Republic of China. Especially the Basic Healthcare and Health Promotion Law from 2019 is worth noting as it gave legal effect to ambitious health reform programs like 'Healthy China 2030'. This Law comprehensively overhauled the health regulatory framework of China and aimed to guarantee basic medical services for all citizens, enhance healthcare delivery and establish a 'Healthy China'. So, in essence this law legally allowed the State to play a much greater role in the healthcare system, ensure basic medical services for every citizen and make sure that all medicines are available at reasonable prices. The new law should ensure that all citizens are entitled to basic medical services provided by the State, including disease prevention, diagnosis, treatment, nursing, rehabilitation and other services delivered with drugs, appropriate technologies and related equipment. Furthermore, these basic medical services are to be provided free of charge, by governments at county level or above, through the establishment of all kinds of professional public health facilities in big cities and small villages alike. The State must also guarantee the supply, safety and effectiveness of essential

---

[2] Library of Congress. 2019. China: Drug administration law revised. www.loc.gov/item/global-legal-monitor/2019-10-31/china-drug-administration-law-revised/. Accessed on September 20, 2023.

drugs and their reasonable prices.[3] One key component under the NHSA is it's responsible for the implementation of the National Reimbursement Drug List (NRDL), which is now the main route for drug reimbursement in China.[4]

The last important government agency is the SAMR which regulates anticompetitive practices such as forming monopolistic agreements and abusing a dominant market position pursuant to the Antitrust Law of the People's Republic of China, amended in 2022 (the Antitrust Law), and supervises anticompetitive behavior such as trade secret misappropriation, commercial bribery and false advertising according to the Anti-Unfair Competition Law of the People's Republic of China, amended in 2019 (the Anti-Unfair Competition Law).[5]

From all these institutions the NMPA is best known as all biopharmaceutical companies which develop drugs, sooner or later will have to deal with this agency. For any company wanting to sell its drugs in China, the NHSA and more importantly its NRDL are the main channel to focus on.

REGULATORY REFORMS AND NEW POLICIES

For a long time, these three China's state agencies were notoriously understaffed, ill equipped and in general completely out of date with international standards and harmonization. For the biopharma sector it meant that there were no clear procedures or framework how to get innovative drugs approved. In the late 1990s it took for instance seven years longer for new drugs to get approval in China than the US or Europe. In 2011 it took 31 months to get a clinical trial application approved in

---

[3] National Library of Medicine. 2021. The political determinants of China's new health constitution. www.ncbi.nlm.nih.gov/pmc/articles/PMC7989297/. Accessed on September 20, 2023.

[4] National Library of Medicine. 2023. Access to innovative drugs and the National Reimbursement Drug List in China: Changing dynamics and future trends in pricing and reimbursement. https://www.ncbi.nlm.nih.gov/pmc/articles/PMC10266112/. Accessed on November 4, 2023.

[5] Lexology. 2023. A general introduction to pharmaceutical IP and competition issues in China. www.lexology.com/library/detail.aspx?g=270ff683-97f3-4af6-992f-ce8 cd9f60922&utm_source=lexology+daily+newsfeed&utm_medium=html+email+-+body+-+ general+section&utm_campaign=lexology+subscriber+daily+feed&utm_content=lexology+ daily+newsfeed+2023-09-19&utm_term_=. Accessed on September 20, 2023.

China. In 2015 China had a backlog of 21,000 drug registrations pending review and approval.[6] Even until 2017, the NMPA still had a multiyear backlog of new drugs awaiting approval.[7] IP protection was also weak which meant that innovative drugs could relatively be easy to be turned into generics.

The result of all this was, that in China for a long time there was no standardized drug approval process noteworthy speaking of. There were no incentives at all for investors nor biopharma companies to engage in innovative drug making, and foreign drugs were not on the market. As a result, Chinese patients often had no access at all to innovative oncology medicines. The government realized that drastic reforms had to be made to get innovation started in the Chinese pharma sector, and to give Chinese citizens access to new life-saving treatments coming from abroad.

The process of reform kicked off in 2015, when the 'Made in China 2025' policy specified biopharmaceuticals as a key sector for development. For the regulatory process, the chief targets to be achieved included improving the drug review process and shortening IND and NDA review timelines, encouraging new drug innovation, eliminating the existing backlog of registration applications and minimizing the drug lag—the time it takes to have a new drug approved in a certain country after it has been approved by other jurisdictions.[8]

The first step was taken in 2016 when China announced a Priority Review System which allowed innovative drugs for rare diseases and urgently needed treatments to be assessed faster. In the same year the 'Healthy China 2030' initiative was launched which stated a long-term vision for healthcare and encouraged innovation. One year later China joined the International Conference on Harmonization of Technical Requirements for Registration of Pharmaceuticals for Human Use (ICH)

---

[6] GreenbergTraurig. 2021. China on the move: An improving regulatory landscape with new challenges ahead—Genomics and national security. https://www.gtlaw.com/en/insights/2021/6/china-on-the-move-an-improving-regulatory-landscape-challenges-genomics-national-security. Accessed on November 9, 2023.

[7] BCG. 2020. Competing in China's booming biopharma market. https://www.bcg.com/publications/2020/competing-in-chinas-biopharma-market. Accessed on November 3, 2023.

[8] Regulatory Focus. 2018. China Regulatory Reform: An update on review times and drug lag. https://www.ppd.com/wp-content/uploads/2020/03/Regulatory-Focus-2018.05-China.pdf. Accessed on November 9, 2023.

which sets the international standards for medicines. That year it also started to update again the National Reimbursement Drug List (NRDL) and introduced the process of price negotiations to get entry on the list. In 2018 the entire process of clinical trials applications started to be reformed with the introduction of the '60-day review' rule which gives regulators two months to assess clinical trial applications. If 60 days pass without a rejection or request for more information, the application is considered approved. Also in 2018, the Volume Based Procurement (VBP) policy was launched. This is a public bidding process for the central procurement of drugs, mainly generics, in an effort to drive down the prices. 2019 saw the introduction of the Marketing Authorization Holder (MAH) system which allows biopharma companies, R&D institutions or researchers to apply for drug market licenses.[9] These were previously only available to enterprises with production licenses. In 2020 the latest version of the Patent Law came out which featured a patent linkage system which allows innovator drug companies to stop generics from obtaining market authorization before patent expiry.

CHINA JOINS ICH

China's joining of the ICH in 2017 was an important milestone in its regulatory history. It signified for the first time that the agency was prepared to adopt ICH technical requirements for drug registration and to become a global player in drug approval and regulation process. The US and Europe encouraged this move to international standards as new members must implement a basic set of regulatory requirements for the manufacturing of pharmaceuticals, the conduct of clinical trials and stability testing of pharmaceutical products.[10]

Since then, NMPA has aligned itself with the ICH guidelines and introduced new concepts, methods, tools and standards of regulation. It generally aligns itself through three principles. The first is to ensure that its own content does not conflict with the ICH guidelines. The second

---

[9] Nikkei Asia. 2022. Pharmacy of the world: China's quest to be the No. 1 drugmaker. https://asia.nikkei.com/static/vdata/infographics/chinavaccine-2/. Accessed on November 5, 2023.

[10] National Library of Medicine. 2022. Trends and characteristics of new drugs approvals in China, 2011–2021. https://www.ncbi.nlm.nih.gov/pmc/articles/PMC9628473/. Accessed on November 5, 2023.

is to fully draw on the guidelines of developed regulatory agencies in Europe (EMEA), the US (FDA) and Japan (PMDA) to ensure that China aligns with international standards. Thirdly it accumulates and shares China's experiences for subsequent international ICH harmonization.[11]

This all had huge implications. By starting to integrate itself globally in the regulatory framework, it basically meant that Western biopharma companies could much easier get access to the Chinese market. They could use protocols and procedures for previously done trials in the US or Europe and use them as a basis to start communications with the Chinese authorities, instead of the need to designing a whole new set of protocols from scratch. It also meant that China now for the first time relatively effortless could be integrated into global trials, which drives down costs a lot, compared to the requirement to do a complete set of independent trials in China. At the same time, it also meant that Chinese companies could also access the Western markets much easier, as foreign regulators would also accept protocols of clinical trials in China.

Drugs Approval and Priority Review System

In the past, it took about 900 days to review and approve a drug registration in China. In 2019 this procedure was shortened to about 300 days, mainly because of an increase in staff at the CDE (Center of Drug Evaluation) which increased from 100 in 2015 to about 1,000 in 2020. Further improvements came in 2020 when the NMPA established clear timelines for the entire drug review and approval process. Under the 2020 Drug Registration Measures, an application for clinical trial is deemed approved by CDE if not objected to by the CDE within 60 working days of CDE's acceptance of such application. The overall time limit for review and approval is in principle 200 working days.[12]

Besides this China also established a Priority Review system. This is a fast-track regulatory program that reduces regulatory review and approval timelines for innovative drugs with significant clinical advantages and for

---

[11] DIA Global Forum. 2021. China focusing innovation through ICH global regulatory vision. https://globalforum.diaglobal.org/issue/august-2021/#regulatoryvision. Accessed on November 5, 2023.

[12] Regulatory Focus. 2018. China Regulatory Reform: an update on review times and drug lag. https://www.ppd.com/wp-content/uploads/2020/03/Regulatory-Focus-2018.05-China.pdf. Accessed on November 9, 2023.

which there is an urgent clinical need. From 2016 onwards China started to reform its regulatory system to include various fast-track programs similar to the US, EU and Japan, in order to incentivize the development of drugs for unmet medical needs and serious conditions. Under this system it became possible to accelerate market access in China, even before the formal regulatory approval of the NMPA. Currently the timeline to get a drug approved under the Priority Review System is 130 days.[13]

China currently follows four programs for accelerating the review and approval of new drug applications (NDA). The first one is breakthrough therapy designation (BTD) for innovative of improved drugs. These drugs are for life-threatening diseases or diseases that seriously impact life quality. Secondly there is conditional approval (CA). This is for drugs which treat serious life-threatening conditions that currently have no effective treatment. This also includes vaccinations which are urgently needed for severe public health emergencies. Thirdly there is the priority review (PR) for drugs in shortage and with urgent clinical needs, or new drugs to prevent and treat serious infectious/rare diseases. Lastly there is the special approval (SA). This is for drugs which treat an ongoing public health problem or after an emergency.[14]

NATIONAL REIMBURSEMENT DRUG LIST (NRDL) AND PRICE NEGOTIATIONS

Market access and reimbursement in China have been a persistent problem in China. The Chinese government historically adopted a price ceiling for pharmaceutical products which meant not all drugs were available, as some of them were deemed too expensive. Furthermore, despite the fact that about 95% of the 1.4 billion Chinese people are covered under the government's public insurance schemes, the coverage was inadequate because of the high out-of-pocket costs for patients and poor

---

[13] Accestra. 2023. China CDE eyes more drug approvals by 2025. https://www.accestra.com/china-cde-eyes-more-drug-approvals-by-2025/. Accessed on November 9, 2023.

[14] Baipharm. 2021. Expedited programs for drugs registration in China. https://baipharm.chemlinked.com/insights/expedited-programs-for-drug-registration-in-china. Accessed on November 5, 2023.

coverage of innovative, premium-priced medicines.[15] Often no innovative targeted anti-cancer drugs or other new medicines launched in China, could be reimbursed, while families had to pay 100% out of their own pocket to get the medicines they needed.[16]

To tackle this problem, China introduced the National Reimbursement Drug List (NRDL) in 2000 and the National Essential Drug List (NEDL) in 2009.[17] Both were intended to support universal healthcare coverage and affordable basic treatment for all citizens. The NRDL and NEDL are the main lists that drug manufacturers may want to enter in China in order to achieve a high number of sales. The NEDL is a list of drugs that have been used for a long time with a high frequency. It is the list of medicines in China that need to be in stock at public hospitals and clinics for treating the most common illnesses. The NEDL list is relevant because Chinese institutions are strongly incentivized to buy drugs on this list. As such drugs on this list will have access to a big market.[18] The NRDL on the other hand includes drugs reimbursable by the public insurance schemes. For innovative drug makers, now the NRDL is the most important list and getting access to it, is of premium importance. Inclusion on the NRDL means that products will be fully or partially reimbursed at a national level. In general they are the only products to be prescribed at public hospitals.

Although the NRDL was meant to be updated every two years, it was updated only twice between 2000 and 2017.[19] This effectively blocked access to many innovative medicines for Chinese patients. Changes were

---

[15] Clarivate. 2019. The evolving dynamics of access and reimbursement in China. https://clarivate.com/blog/evolving-dynamics-access-reimbursement-china/. Accessed on September 20, 2023.

[16] World Health Organization. 2023. Expanding access to high-quality medicines. https://www.who.int/china/activities/expanding-access-to-high-quality-medicines. Accessed on September 20, 2023.

[17] Clarivate. 2019. The evolving dynamics of access and reimbursement in China. https://clarivate.com/blog/evolving-dynamics-access-reimbursement-china/. Accessed on September 20, 2023.

[18] Pacific Bridge Medical. 2023. Reimbursement and market access for drugs. www.pacificbridgemedical.com/regulatory-services/pharmaceutical/reimbursement/reimbursement-for-pharmaceuticals-in-china/. Accessed on November 5, 2023.

[19] Clarivate. 2019. The evolving dynamics of access and reimbursement in China. https://clarivate.com/blog/evolving-dynamics-access-reimbursement-china/. Accessed on September 20, 2023.

needed and after eight years of no updates, China agreed in 2017 that as part of the Healthy China 2030 policy the NRDL would be updated annually. Now NRDL is the main gateway and the only reimbursement list for patented drugs.[20] Regular updates of the list were being started from 2017, and its yearly new additions included more and more innovative drugs. From 2015 China also started to explore a price negotiation mechanism to make drug prices affordable to public funding. They landed on a system where hospitals buy drugs from pharma companies at a price pre-negotiated with the government, which reimburses most of the cost. That system effectively started in 2017 at the third NRDL update when negotiations started with the manufacturers of certain therapies for price discounts in exchange for inclusion in NRDL's list of innovative medicines.[21] Since then, the NRDL has expanded significantly and has become the standard for pricing in China.

Although initially the negotiation process was being lauded by multinational manufacturers as well as China's patient and physician community as a great initiative to improve access to innovative therapies, at the same time, manufacturers found the system not very transparent and hard to navigate. In the early years for instance there was no formal process to apply for a drug's inclusion in the NRDL. Drugs were selected by government officials and expert advisory committees comprising physicians and pharma experts, but without any input from manufacturers. Moreover, further negotiations for the selected drugs were only held if the manufacturer-offered price was 15% below the undisclosed price set by the committee.[22] That meant manufacturers could only guess what pricing the government was aiming at.

Gradually, however, the system has been improved. The NRDL pricing methodology and negotiation period have been more established and standardized, and pharmaceutical companies are now more used to the

---

[20] PharmaEx. 2022. The emergences of commercial health insurances as an access route to the Chinese market. www.pharmexec.com/view/emergence-commercial-health-insurances-access-route-chinese-market. Accessed on September 20, 2023.

[21] Clarivate. 2019. The evolving dynamics of access and reimbursement in China. https://clarivate.com/blog/evolving-dynamics-access-reimbursement-china/. Accessed on September 20, 2023.

[22] Clarivate. 2019. The evolving dynamics of access and reimbursement in China. https://clarivate.com/blog/evolving-dynamics-access-reimbursement-china/. Accessed on September 20, 2023.

mechanism. The NHSA, together with other governmental authorities, annually reviews the inclusion or removal of drugs from the NRDL, decides on the tier under which a drug is classified, and considers factors, including clinical necessity, price and efficacy in its determination. Then the NHSA initiates several rounds of price negotiations with manufacturers of patented drugs, drugs with an exclusive source of supply and oncology drugs. Pharmaceutical companies are free to set prices for their pharmaceutical products (other than narcotic and Type 1 psychotropic drugs).[23] Drugs are listed on the NRDL and qualified for purchase by public hospitals once the price is agreed with the drugmaker. Steep cuts in prices are needed to get access to the list. Since the start of the regular updates of the NRDL, a successful price negotiation often results in a 40–50% price reduction from the original price proposed by pharmaceutical companies.[24]

The NRDL and its price negotiations are now well established as the sole route to public funding in China and the main pathway for any pharmaceutical looking for reimbursement. Pharmaceutical drugs listed are divided into Class A and Class B pharmaceuticals. Class A pharmaceuticals are drugs widely used in clinical treatment with good efficacy and lower prices in a specific category. The drugs are considered to be essential and affordable and are fully reimbursable. Class B pharmaceuticals are drugs available for clinical treatment with good efficacy and higher prices than Class A pharmaceuticals in a specific category. These drugs are innovative patented drugs and relatively more expensive drugs, or drugs from an exclusive source of supply. They also have specific supply prices agreed between the government and pharmaceutical companies during the NRDL price negotiations. In contrast with Class A Pharmaceuticals, Class B Pharmaceutical drugs are partially reimbursable.[25]

---

[23] Thomson Reuters Practical Law. 2023. Life Sciences commercialization in China: Overview. https://uk.practicallaw.thomsonreuters.com/0-568-3025?transitionType=Default&contextData=(sc.Default)&firstPage=true#co_anchor_a396730. Accessed on November 4, 2023.

[24] Trinity Life Sciences. 2023. Highlights of the National Reimbursement Drug List (NRDL) negotiation outcome. https://trinitylifesciences.com/blog/highlights-of-the-2022-national-reimbursement-drug-list-nrdl-negotiation-outcome/. Accessed on November 29, 2023.

[25] Thomson Reuters Practical Law. 2023. Life Sciences commercialization in China: Overview. https://uk.practicallaw.thomsonreuters.com/0-568-3025?transitionType=Default&contextData=(sc.Default)&firstPage=true#co_anchor_a396730. Accessed on November 4, 2023.

Volume Based Procurement (VBP)

In 2018 China launched a new round of drug pricing and procurement reforms with a focus on generic drugs. The aim was to lower the price of drug for patients, reduce transaction costs for enterprises, regulate drug use by hospitals and improve the centralized drug procurement and pricing system.[26] As it was well known that hospitals and pharma companies asked for premium prices for many drugs, the government launched the so-called volume-based procurement (VBP) policy in essence to force pharmaceutical companies into lowering drug prices. The main principle of VBP is to trade high volumes for lower prices. A significant threshold is in place as VBP only starts when the specific drug sales in China reach about US$70 million.[27]

The volume-based procurement of drugs is open to all enterprises that manufacture drugs and are listed on the government procurement list. The buyers—public hospitals—are encouraged to form a group procurement organization, in order to get the cheapest price. Since its introduction, sometimes significant price reductions up to 80 or 90% of the original price are needed to win a bid in the VBP.[28]

Marketing Authorization Holder (MAH)

In 2019 the government approved a nationwide drug Marketing Authorization Holder system (MAH). The MAH refers to the enterprise, drug research institution, or other entity, which obtains a drug registration certificate in China. The MAH requires that the holder of a drug marketing authorization will be responsible for the safety, efficacy and

---

[26] Thomson Reuters Practical Law. 2023. Life Sciences commercialization in China: overview. https://uk.practicallaw.thomsonreuters.com/0-568-3025?transitionType=Default&contextData=(sc.Default)&firstPage=true#co_anchor_a396730. Accessed on November 4, 2023.

[27] Pacific Bridge Medical. 2023. China announced 8th pharmaceutical national volume based procurement (VBP). https://www.pacificbridgemedical.com/news-brief/china-announces-8th-national-volume-based-procurement-vbp/. Accessed on November 5, 2023.

[28] Reuters. Drugmakers slash prices to win China's bulk-buy contracts: State media. www.reuters.com/article/us-china-drugs-idUSKBN25G1IX/. Accessed on November 29, 2023.

quality control of the drug throughout the entire process of the drug's development, production, distribution, marketing and use.[29]

The system allows the MAH to license manufacturing of drugs to another company. Foreign firms can be the MAH in China, but they have to fulfill their MAH obligations through a Chinese partner, which means that foreign innovative drug developers can obtain a drug registration certificate in China even if the company does not have production facilities in China.[30] This system has significant advantages, notably that it lowers the threshold of entrance to the market as it enables R&D companies to focus on innovation, while production companies can focus on manufacturing. Foreign companies can simply designate a MAH to conduct clinical trials and commercialize their drug in China. MAHs can be either a local legal entity or manufacturer, a medical research institution or a biotech company, or a CRO or CDMO.[31]

Chinese IP Law

The biopharma sector lives and breathes with IP. Almost all biotechs' core—and often only—strength is their R&D and own proprietary technology. Within the sector, considering the market exclusivity it provides and the generous profits it further implies, strong patent laws are major incentives for innovation. As China had a reputation for IP theft, one of the main questions that often needs answering is related to IP protection in China. For biopharma companies, there needs to be sufficient IP protection, before even considering moving into a certain market. Realizing that patents are crucial, China has improved its IP protection system greatly. Over the years China has mostly harmonized its patent legislation with other countries. There has been an overall strengthening of the patent system, and since the establishment of the Patent Law of the

---

[29] Library of Congress. 2019. China: Drug administration law revised. www.loc.gov/item/global-legal-monitor/2019-10-31/china-drug-administration-law-revised/. Accessed on September 20, 2023.

[30] Government of Canada. 2023. Intellectual property protection for pharmaceutical companies in China. www.tradecommissioner.gc.ca/china-chine/market-facts-faits-sur-le-marche/0003690.aspx?lang=eng. Accessed on September 20, 2023.

[31] Clinical Trials Arena. 2022. New territories: Challenges and benefits for western biotechs in China. www.clinicaltrialsarena.com/sponsored/new-territories-challenges-and-benefits-for-western-biotechs-in-china/. Accessed on November 3, 2023.

People's Republic of China (the Patent Law) in 1984, the patent law system has been reviewed and upgraded. Despite the enhanced IP law however, there is still room for further improvement in execution and enforcement.

But by and large, IP is now well protected in China. In fact, Chinese biopharma companies or healthcare investors will only deal with foreign biopharmas if their IP is well protected. Companies which have weak IP protection, should not even consider engaging with Chinese parties. If IP is not protected well, Chinese companies—and certainly not investors—are generally not interested to start even partnering or investment discussions. It is therefore essential to understand the differences in IP protection in different regions. There are notable differences here. Reformulation of existing drugs, for instance, in China is less protected than in other countries.

In China pharmaceutical patents can include both products and methods. You can also patent chemical components, new methods, new applications, derivatives and combinations.[32] However generally speaking you cannot patent methods for diagnosis or treatment of diseases. Doctors in China are given the freedom to choose any way of diagnosing or treating diseases. Since these methods are practiced directly on living humans or animal bodies, they are not inventions-creations according to China patent law. Therefore, methods for the diagnosis or treatment of diseases shall not be granted patent rights.[33] Under the current Patent Law invention patents—once granted by the China National Intellectual Property Administration (CNIPA)—have a protection term of 20 years from its filing date.[34] For generic drug companies, the current Chinese patent law has a regulation equivalent to the 'Bolar Exception' in the US patent system. Generic drug companies can use or import patented

---

[32] Government of Canada. 2023. Intellectual property protection for pharmaceutical companies in China. www.tradecommissioner.gc.ca/china-chine/market-facts-faits-sur-le-marche/0003690.aspx?lang=eng. Accessed on September 20, 2023.

[33] Patenttrademarkblog. 2023. China patent law: Are treatments for diseases patentable? www.patenttrademarkblog.com/china-treatments-diseases/. Accessed on September 20, 2023.

[34] Lexology. 2023. A general introduction to pharmaceutical IP and competition issues in China. www.lexology.com/library/detail.aspx?g=270ff683-97f3-4af6-992f-ce8cd9f60922&utm_source=lexology+daily+newsfeed&utm_medium=html+email+-+body+-+general+section&utm_campaign=lexology+subscriber+daily+feed&utm_content=lexology+daily+newsfeed+2023-09-19&utm_term_=. Accessed on September 20, 2023.

drugs for the purpose of obtaining regulatory approval to register a drug, without this being considered patent infringement.[35]

Truly relevant for the pharmaceutical industry is the 2021 introduction of a completely new patent term extension system for pharmaceutical products. This extension system was aimed to benefit pharmaceutical innovators that are active in China and allow for a compensation of the regulatory delay and significant time required to bring new drugs to the market. The mechanism is strongly inspired by the Patent Term Extension (PTE) system in the US and the similar Supplementary Protection Certificates (SPCs) in Europe, but there are significant differences as well. The overall PTE duration is restricted to 5 years after normal patent expiry or 14 years after marketing authorization (MA). The PTE must be requested at the latest 6 months before patent expiry, which is stricter than the European system (just before patent expiry) or the US system (before patent expiry, but extensions are available).[36] However, for a product to be eligible for a patent extension it is important to note that the product must not have already been approved or marketed in any other country, when MA request is filed in China.[37] Besides the PTE one can also apply for Patent Term Adjustment (PTA). An invention patent granted more than four years after the filing date, and more than three years after submitting the substantive examination request, can be adjusted to compensate for unreasonable delays in the patent examination by the CNIPA.[38] Another notable adjustment in the Patent Law was the patent linkage system, which links generic drug applications to pharmaceutical patent protection, similar to the Hatch–Waxman Act in

---

[35] Government of Canada. 2023. Intellectual property protection for pharmaceutical companies in China. www.tradecommissioner.gc.ca/china-chine/market-facts-faits-sur-le-marche/0003690.aspx?lang=eng. Accessed on September 20, 2023.

[36] Gevers. 2023. Patent term extensions now available in China. www.gevers.eu/blog/patents/patent-term-extensions-now-available-in-china. Accessed on September 20, 2023.

[37] Plasseraud. 2022. Patent term extension in China is not possible for pharmaceutical patents. www.plass.com/en/articles/patent-term-extension-china-now-possible-pharmaceutical-patents. Accessed on September 20, 2023.

[38] Thomson Reuters Practical Law. 2023. Life sciences commercialization in China: Overview. https://uk.practicallaw.thomsonreuters.com/0-568-3025?transitionType=Default&contextData=(sc.Default)&firstPage=true#co_anchor_a713776. Accessed on September 20, 2023.

the US.[39] Under this new system, innovator drug companies can stop generics from obtaining market authorization before patent expiry.

REAL-WORLD EVIDENCE

The traditional way of developing medicines and testing them on patients is to conduct large long-term studies on real patients with real-world conditions and then publish their findings. These clinical trials are tightly controlled studies in which participants are given specific interventions according to a protocol to evaluate their safety and efficacy. Clinical trials are not only very costly, but also take a long time to do. Real-world evidence (RWE) on the other hand is a method of gathering information from medical records and other sources. In RWE patient data are generated outside of clinical studies and have been shown to improve the quality and cost-effectiveness of healthcare. The term 'real-world' refers to how patients interact with their healthcare system, something that is not always easy to study for researchers.[40] Therefore, RWE is a powerful tool for answering questions that are difficult to study in clinical trials.

Over the past decade, RWE has been increasingly recognized for its value in many markets, but in China this is a far more recent phenomenon. Real-world evidence is however playing an increasingly vital role in China, ranging from early access and regulatory approval to reimbursement listing and commercialization. The RWE regulatory landscape in China has been dynamic and rapidly evolving, with the NMPA leading this trend into drugs for pediatrics and other special populations.[41] It was from 2019 on that RWE started to gain momentum in China. In September of that year the subtropical island of Hainan pioneered an RWE pilot program as first region in China in its Boao Lecheng International Medical Tourism Pilot Zone. The years after the NMPA published

[39] PwC. 2022. New China patent linkage system for pharmaceuticals and biologics. www.pwccn.com/en/industries/life-sciences-and-healthcare/publications/new-china-patent-linkage-system-jul2022.html. Accessed on September 20, 2023.

[40] Vial. 2023. What is real-world evidence in clinical trials? https://vial.com/blog/articles/what-is-real-world-evidence-in-clinical-trials/?https://vial.com/blog/articles/what-is-real-world-evidence-in-clinical-trials/?utm_source=organic. Accessed on November 18, 2023.

[41] Global Forum. 2022. Real-world evidence regulatory landscape in Asia Pacific: Australia, China, Japan, South Korea, and Taiwan. https://globalforum.diaglobal.org/issue/june-2022/#regulatorylandscape. Accessed on November 18, 2023.

new guidelines on how to obtain and use RWE data.[42] In all these guidelines, the NMPA and the CDE highlighted specific circumstances for which RWE could bring unique value to the development and approval process. As the RWE pioneer, by 2022 the Hainan studies had led to the approval of one drug—Gavreto—which was marketed in China nine months after its FDA approval.

Despite all this the systematic use of RWE to support drug regulatory decision-making, is still in its infancy in China. Until now Haian is the only region in China that can use licensed medical devices and drugs that have been approved in other countries but not registered in China. By July 2022, a total of 24 licensed imported drugs and medical devices had been included in the RWD application pilot of Hainan. Among them, eight products have since been approved for market, including three drugs.[43] Currently in China RWE can increase approvals for products involving rare diseases, pediatric diseases where the diseases progress quickly or are life-threatening, various surgical procedures that are difficult to perform, etc. In addition to Hainan Island, RWE can be helpful for approvals in the Greater Bay Area, and in the Shanghai Pudong Free Trade Zone. For product reimbursement, RWE can help payers better determine the value of innovative treatments. RWE provides valuable information on long-term benefits and thus helps payers determine real economic benefits.[44]

The systematic use of RWE to support drug regulatory decision-making may be still an early-stage venture, but its use is growing exponentially. Regulatory authorities, partnering with industry, academia and medical institutions, are positively driving forward the applications of RWE. It is expected that China will increasingly apply new artificial intelligence technologies, such as natural language processing and machine learning in RWE, and as such drive it forward rapidly.

---

[42] PharmaExec. 2022. Real-world evidence is becoming a pivotal component in Chinese healthcare. https://www.pharmexec.com/view/real-world-evidence-is-becoming-a-pivotal-component-in-chinese-healthcare. Accessed on November 18, 2023.

[43] Springer. Therapeutic innovation & Regulatory science. 2023. https://link.springer.com/article/10.1007/s43441-023-00555-9 Accessed on November 18, 2023.

[44] PharmaExec. 2022. Real-world evidence is becoming a pivotal component in Chinese healthcare. https://www.pharmexec.com/view/real-world-evidence-is-becoming-a-pivotal-component-in-chinese-healthcare. Accessed on November 18, 2023.

China Has Integrated Globally

The major reforms, initiated in 2015 have significantly improved all aspects of the biopharmaceutical sector. Major hurdles have been removed. The improved procedures to accelerate new-drug reviews for instance, including raising the number of staff at the Center for Drug Evaluation (CDE) from 150 in 2015 to more than 700 in 2018, helped clear a backlog of 20,000 applications in two years.[45] In terms of timelines, between 2017 and 2021, the median drug approval time was 15.4 months.[46] In the regulatory field, by 2023 China had implemented 100% of the remaining ICH guidelines. This is undoubtedly a milestone achievement, as it greatly improves market access for foreign companies, and helps Chinese companies to venture outside China. By translating and implementing ICH guidelines from 2017 on, the NMPA has made very positive changes to China's drug regulatory system and to the consequent innovation of China's drug development sector.

Most importantly of all there are very visible and positive results for Chinese patients. They have much more access to innovative medicines than ever before. As regulations were streamlined between 2017 and 2021, foreign and Chinese biopharma companies started to bring in drugs as never before. The number of drug applications increased from 4,839 to 11,658, an average annual increase by 24,59%.[47] Between 2011 and 2021 a total of 353 new drugs were approved. The annual number of new drug approvals especially increased dramatically since 2017, reaching a record high of 70 in 2021.

There are, however, still challenges. Drug lag for instance remains an issue. The FDA approved a total of 219 new products between 2015 and 2019, but only 40 of them had been approved in China by the end of

---

[45] McKinsey & Co. 2021. The dawn of China biopharma innovation. https://www.mckinsey.com/industries/life-sciences/our-insights/the-dawn-of-china-biopharma-innovation. Accessed on October 26, 2023.

[46] National Library of Medicine. 2022. Trends and characteristics of new drugs approvals in China, 2011–2021. https://www.ncbi.nlm.nih.gov/pmc/articles/PMC9628473/. Accessed on November 5, 2023.

[47] Accestra. 2023. China CDE eyes more drug approvals by 2025. https://www.accestra.com/china-cde-eyes-more-drug-approvals-by-2025/. Accessed on November 9, 2023.

2019.[48] So, while the review and approval of drugs in China has sped up notably since the regulatory reform in 2015, it's clear that reducing the long-standing drug lag will take a considerable time. Even in 2022, only 25% of FDA approved drugs, are approved in China. So, despite the work done, China's regulatory system still needs some improvements. The CDE has announced that between 2021 and 2025 there will be 300 new or revised technical guidelines. It is expected that by 2025 the total number of technical guidelines for drugs will surpass 600.[49] As such China will keep on working on improving its regulatory environment in the foreseeable future and implement the latest international standards and regulations.

[48] Global Forum. 2020. New drug approvals in China in 2019. https://globalforum.diaglobal.org/issue/may-2020/new-drug-approvals-in-china-in-2019/. Accessed on November 9, 2023.

[49] Accestra. 2023. China CDE eyes more drug approvals by 2025. https://www.accestra.com/china-cde-eyes-more-drug-approvals-by-2025/. Accessed on November 9, 2023.

The Golden Age of Chinese Biopharma Sector, 2014–2021: Explosive Growth in a Thriving Ecosystem

Abstract The Chinese biopharma sector has witnessed an unprecedented growth, referred to as the 'Golden Age'. A combination of factors has nurtured this explosive domestic growth in the pharma and biotech space. With the largest population in the world and with little access to the latest innovative medicines, China provided huge market opportunities. Regulatory reforms made approval of new drugs much easier, which led to venture capitalists eying the Chinese biopharma sector as new growth sector. The government streamlined the clinical trial and drug approval process, including priority and special reviews as well as breakthrough therapy designations for innovative products that target unmet medical needs in China. The NRDL is also being updated more frequently and prioritizes the entry of newly approved novel drugs. Then there is also the huge number of hospitals which provide a massive set of potential patients to enroll into clinical trials. New capital sources became available, when in 2018 changes in policy allowed pre-revenue/pre-profit biotech companies to be listed in the Hong Kong Stock Exchange (HKEX) or Shanghai Stock Exchange's Science and Technology Innovative Board (STAR). Combined together, all of these factors can be seen as the rocket booster for growth, which fueled the Golden Age of the Chinese biopharma sector.

Keywords Venture capital (VC) · Biotechnology · Clinical trials · Contract research organization (CRO) · Contract development and manufacturing organization (CDMO) · Hong Kong Stock Exchange (HKEX) · In-licensing · Research & Development (R&D) · Sea turtles · Shanghai Stock Exchange's Science and Technology Innovative Board (STAR)

The Chinese biopharma sector has witnessed an unprecedented growth. The ones who lived through it, often referred to it as the 'Golden Age'. A combination of factors has nurtured this explosive domestic growth in the pharma and biotech space. With the largest population in the world and with little access to the latest innovative medicines, China provided huge market opportunities. Regulatory reforms made approval of new drugs much easier, which led to venture capitalists eyeing the Chinese biopharma sector as a new growth sector. The NMPA has streamlined the clinical trial and drug approval process, including priority and special reviews as well as breakthrough therapy designations for innovative products that target unmet medical needs in China. The NRDL is also being updated more frequently and prioritizes the entry of newly approved novel drugs.

Then there is also the huge number of hospitals which provide a massive set of potential patients to enroll into clinical trials. New capital sources became available, when in 2018 changes in policy allowed pre-revenue/pre-profit biotech companies to be listed in the Hong Kong Stock Exchange (HKEX) or Shanghai Stock Exchange's Science and Technology Innovative Board (STAR). Combined together, all of these factors can be seen as the rocket booster for growth, which fueled the Golden Age of the Chinese biopharma sector.

Venture Capitalists Move in

The 'Made in China 2025' policy which specified biopharmaceuticals as a key sector for development and its consequent regulatory reforms, didn't go unnoticed by specialized healthcare venture capitalists. Sensing a once in a lifetime opportunity, venture capital started to shift to the Chinese healthcare sector and kicked-off the investments in the space.

The momentous shift from a formerly generics-focused play toward innovative medicines, attracted astronomical amounts of capital. The data vary depending on the parameters used, but the numbers are impressive. In 2018 McKinsey estimated that the total amount of cash available through PE/VC healthcare funds reached US$40 billion in 2017, up from US$4 billion in 2014. That is a whopping ten times increase in just three years. The number of funds also increased significantly, from 48 in 2014 to 74 in 2017. During the same period, the average size of the funds had ballooned from US$83 million to around US$540 million.[1] According to ChinaBio, venture capital funding in 2020 had surged for healthcare startups in China, with roughly US$60 billion invested since 2015.[2] We ourselves estimate that in 2021, at the height of the investment mania, there were about 300 healthcare funds.

For the biopharma sector this meant that venture capital was readily available to be invested into biotech companies. Venture-capital funding to the biopharma space tripled to US$12 billion in 2018–2020 from US$4 billion in 2015–2017.[3] That made China the second-largest source of biopharma funding in the world, behind the US.[4] The number of investment deals reached 478 in 2017, up from 64 in 2014. This implies in 2017 an average investment of roughly US$25 million per deal.[5]

---

[1] McKinsey & Co. 2018. Investors are plowing billions of dollars into China's rapidly growing healthcare market. Here's why. https://www.mckinsey.com/cn/our-insights/perspectives-on-china-blog/investors-are-plowing-billions-of-dollars-into-chinas-rapidly-growing-healthcare-market-heres-why. Accessed om November 26, 2023.

[2] Capital Group. 2020. China's biopharma industry moves closer to inflection point. https://www.capitalgroup.com/institutional/insights/articles/china-biopharma-stocks.html. Accessed on November 21, 2023.

[3] McKinsey & Co. 2022. Vision 2028: how China could impact the global biopharma industry. https://www.mckinsey.com/~/media/mckinsey/industries/life%20sciences/our%20insights/vision%202028%20how%20china%20could%20impact%20the%20global%20biopharma%20industry/vision-2028-how-china-could-impact-the-global-biopharma-industry.a. Accessed on November 24, 2023.

[4] Silicon Valley Bank. 2020. China in the global healthcare system. www.svb.com/globalassets/library/managedassets/pdfs/china-global-healthcare-report-2020.pdf. Accessed on November 24, 2023.

[5] McKinsey & Co. 2018. Investors are plowing billions of dollars into China's rapidly growing healthcare market. Here's why. https://www.mckinsey.com/cn/our-insights/perspectives-on-china-blog/investors-are-plowing-billions-of-dollars-into-chinas-rapidly-growing-healthcare-market-heres-why. Accessed on November 26, 2023.

In the period 2018–2020 also China started to see an increase in big investment rounds. In 2018 alone there were three US$250M+ deals: Genor Biopharma, Brii Biosciences and CStone Pharmaceuticals.

2018–2020 Deals

Source Silicon Valley Bank, 2020. China in the global healthcare system

In the period 2018–2021 the money deployed even grew bigger. Startup biopharma companies which raised an A-Series funding of US$50 million and B-Series funding of US$100 million were no exception at all.

From all the places in China to raise money, Shanghai is the place to be. Shanghai dominates China's healthcare funding with US$7.2 billion, raised by companies between the period 2018–2020. To put that in perspective, San Francisco -the second highest-funded city in the world in terms of US$ venture-backed healthcare investment- raised US$7.4 billion during the same period. According to the Silicon Valley Bank, over 60% of Shanghai's healthcare investment has gone toward biopharma. Beijing trails Shanghai in overall funding and deals with healthcare funding of US$3.7 billion. This is only half the amount of the healthcare funding of Shanghai, but almost the same amount as the funding in France (US$2.3 billion) and Germany (US$1.7 billion) venture backed investments combined.[6]

---

[6] Silicon Valley Bank. 2020. China in the global healthcare system. www.svb.com/global assets/library/managedassets/pdfs/china-global-healthcare-report-2020.pdf. Accessed on November 24, 2023.

$1B+ Regions for Healthcare Innovation
VC Deals and Dollars, 2018–2020

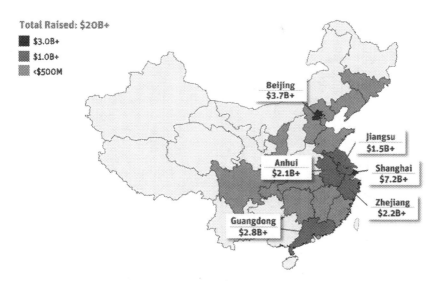

Source Silicon Valley, 2020. China in the global healthcare system

Most investments in the Chinese biopharma sector were done by Chinese investors. Renowned names like Lily Asia Ventures, Lighthouse Capital, Qiming Ventures or IDG Capital were involved in many investment rounds. American venture capitalist healthcare funds also invested in China, but mainly when there was a Western company involved. European investors were slow to catchup. European healthcare funds like Forbion and Soffinova have since years looked at the emerging China biopharma market, but didn't invest (much). Novo Holdings from Denmark is a rare example. In 2023 it still participated in a US$290 million investment round in Chinese life sciences research enabler Sangon Biotech.[7]

---

[7] Fiercepharma. 2023. Carvykti gains momentum; Novo joins Sangon funding round; China calls for foreign investmenthttps://www.fiercepharma.com/pharma/carvyktis-momentum-novos-funding-sangon-chinas-call-foreign-investment. Accessed on November 25, 2023.

Most Active Investors
Number of Deals (Mainland China and Hong Kong, 2018–2020)

Venture Capital (HQ'd in China / HK)		Venture Capital (HQ'd outside of China / HK)		Corporate Investor	
59	QIMING	11	F-PRIME	17	Legend Star
35	SEQUOIA CAPITAL CHINA	11	OrbiMed	16	WuXi AppTec
27	Lilly Asia Ventures	8	EIGHT ROADS	13	Baidu
23	LEGEND CAPITAL	7	ARCH VENTURE PARTNERS	12	FOSUN PHARMA
22	Highlight Capital	6	DECHENG CAPITAL	12	SBCVC
22	matrix	6	EMERGING Technology Partners	12	BGI
22	Shenzhen Capital Group	6	SOSV	11	Tencent
21	IDG Capital	5*	VIVO	9	CMB International

Source Silicon Valley Bank, 2020. China in the global healthcare system

Chinese companies on the rise also obtained international investment from foreign biopharma companies. Merck invested already in BeiGene in 2011, more than three years before its US$75 million A-series funding.[8] In 2019 Amgen acquired a 20.5% stake in BeiGene, which was up by US$1.5 billion two years later. In 2020, Pfizer invested US$200 million in Cstone Pharmaceuticals and gained access to the latter's late-stage oncology drug in mainland China.[9] Because of the Chinese and global downturn, foreign investments in the Chinese biopharma space have however decreased since 2022.

---

[8] FiercePharma. 2020. 10 biotechs to know in China. https://www.fiercepharma.com/special-report/10-biotechs-to-know-china. Accessed on November 26, 2023.

[9] China Briefing. 2022. China's biopharma industry: market prospects, investment paths. https://www.china-briefing.com/news/china-booming-biopharmaceuticals-market-innovation-investment-opportunities/. Accessed on November 15, 2023.

European and North American investment in Chinese pharma market 2013-2023 ($m)

Despite generally rising deal values throughout the last nine years, 2022 had a drop in Western investment.

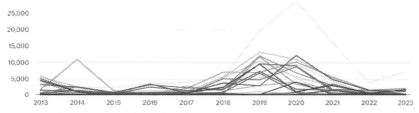

Source Pharmaceutical technology. 2023. Signal: Chinese economic slump hurts pharma firms invested in the region

The Sea Turtles Return Home

Money is one thing, but having the right talents to utilize it properly is quite another. It is well-known that China has a large pool of talent. In 2020 Chinese universities produced around 150,000 life-sciences graduates annually, compared with America's 137,000.[10] But despite all this knowledge, in the biopharma sector there was a lack of experienced people who had built a biopharma company, ran clinical trials, or were deeply involved in drug development. Within the mature and traditional Chinese pharma companies it was also hard to find experienced staff as almost all of them were producing generic medicines, and not innovative medicines. There was in other words a lack of C-level executives, project managers and experienced people in general who could drive biotech companies to success. So as these talents could not be found at home, government and venture capitalists alike ventured abroad to attract talent.

In the 1980s and 90s many Chinese scientists left China to study abroad. Not only was education better in the US or Europe, but there were also better career opportunities. The US especially benefited greatly from this influx of talent. Many of these talents built a career there, and

---

[10] Information Technology and Innovation Foundation. 2020. The impact of China's policies on global biopharmaceutical industry innovation. https://itif.org/publications/2020/09/08/impact-chinas-policies-global-biopharmaceutical-industry-innovation/

at the same time became very well trained and versed in the international biopharma sector standards. As many of these so-called 'sea turtles' held senior management or research positions in Western multinationals or biopharma companies, they had experience from both the commercial and regulatory side. This talent was now very welcome to inject some much-needed expertise in the emerging Chinese biopharma sector. From their side the many Chinese scientists who studied and worked for long periods of time abroad—mostly holding US passports—suddenly spotted vast opportunities to tap into a booming market and set up their own biotechs.

The Chinese government also launched policies to attract these talents. With the aim of making the country a global leader in science and technology, China launched around 200 plans to attract talent to China. The Thousand Talents Plan launched in 2008 recruited approximately 60,000 overseas professionals between 2008 and 2016 to return to China to work.[11] The vast majority of the ones who returned to China were overseas Chinese experts. The Thousand Talents Plan offered them significant incentives. The ones that returned may be exempt from the hukou system which governs where people may live and work. Some were paid huge signing bonuses of up to US$145,000, received work visas for their family members, and could obtain positions at world-class universities in China.[12] It has been estimated that over a ten-year period, the plan cost China between US$ 550 million and US$1.1 billion.[13] The geopolitical tensions between the US and China accelerated the return back home of Chinese scientists also. As the US Department of Justice under its 'China Initiative' targeted researchers at US universities in a bid to combat the theft of intellectual property, many Chinese scientists felt increasingly unwelcome in the US.

---

[11] Biospace. 2022. Why China's biotech sector thrives despite a global recession. https://www.biospace.com/article/why-china-s-biotech-sector-thrives-despite-a-global-recession-/. Accessed on September 8, 2023.

[12] Foreign Policy Magazine, 2020. If you want to keep talent out of China, invest at home. https://foreignpolicy.com/2020/09/17/china-thousand-talents-plan-invest-us-xenophobia/. Accessed on September 8, 2023.

[13] Foreign Policy Magazine, 2020. If you want to keep talent out of China, invest at home. https://foreignpolicy.com/2020/09/17/china-thousand-talents-plan-invest-us-xenophobia/. Accessed on September 8, 2023.

While the government has actively encouraged their return, the attractive market dynamics quickly overtook government incentives. C-level executives in Chinese biopharma companies often enjoy higher salaries than their US counterparts, while there were regularly new opportunities to change jobs and even earn more money. It was widespread practice that talented and experienced Chinese staff from Western Big Pharma companies were approached by the numerous Chinese healthcare investment funds, to set up new companies, funded by the venture capitalists. Deep-pocketed startups were poaching top talent from multinationals. Companies like Sanofi, Merck and GSK saw a brain drain of talents. Many left the big multinationals to set up their own companies or join fast-growing startups in China. Funded by venture capitalists, companies like BeiGene, Innovent Biologics, Hua Medicine, Junshi Biosciences, Zai Lab, Cstone Pharmaceuticals, I-Mab Biopharma and Harbour Biomed were all set up by experienced returnees between 2010 and 2016.

In the biopharma sector the plan definitely paid off dividends and benefited significantly from the skills of these Western-trained Chinese returnees. Returnees have been without question the key driver behind the formation of innovation companies in China over the past decade. In 2020 more than 75% of the top talent in China had at least five years of overseas research experience.[14] They helped the Chinese biopharma industry to rapidly reach international standards of quality, compliance and good manufacturing. The Chinese entrepreneurs from their side were full of energy and ambition. More than once it was coined that this was a unique moment in the Chinese biopharma sector. For them it was an opportunity not to miss. At the same time, they also held high aspirations of transforming access to innovative healthcare for their fellow Chinese.

[14] BCG. 2020. Competing in China's booming biopharma market. https://www.bcg.com/publications/2020/competing-in-chinas-biopharma-market. Accessed on November 3, 2023.

Source Nikkei Asia. Pharmacy of the world: China's quest to be the No. 1 drugmaker. 2021

Talent is key to pushing toward the next level of innovation, and the tide of human capital is shifting. A historic brain drain of scientists leaving China for the US and Europe is becoming a brain gain. Many in the field have returned to China; others never left, given the growing number of promising opportunities. Deep-pocketed startups are poaching top talent from multinationals and compensation packages have risen dramatically for some key roles. These returnees also played a key role in the regulatory reforms undertaken by the NMPA. Because the Chinese regulatory authorities had so little experience in rolling out new guidelines, they tapped into the knowledge and experience of these experienced sea turtles.[15] So, in effect the Chinese industry leaders had a highly active say in shaping the new structure and processes within the NMPA.

China Biotech Model 1.0: In-Licensing to Create Value Quickly

China had plenty of capital, favorable policies and talents returning from abroad. But the Chinese biopharma sector didn't have the core R&D capabilities needed to develop global competitive drugs. This is in stark contrast with almost all US or European biotech startups, which are

---

[15] STAT. 2018. 'It's breathtaking': a Chinese CEO biotech weighs in on policy changes remaking China's FDA. Accessed on November 29, 2023.

heavily R&D focused, and have their own proprietary technology. To overcome this problem and in order to capitalize quickly on the rapidly emerging opportunities in the sector, almost all newly set up biotechs—and to a lesser extent the existing pharma companies which started to focus in innovative medicines—, adopted a very unique business model. As R&D takes a long time and the Chinese market needed quickly a great deal of new medicines, the idea was to find first good drugs—commercialized or under development—abroad, license them in for the Chinese market, do clinical trials in China and commercialize them as soon as possible. This model promised a quick return of investment to the shareholders. In-licensing molecules developed elsewhere is a low-risk path to quickly generate cash flow. At the same time the company would start their own research and development activities, and develop its own assets, to ensure long-term growth and value. The revenue from the in-licensed drugs could then support operations before its self-developed drugs could reach the market.

So in contrast with US and European investors, Chinese venture capitalists didn't focus necessarily on companies which had their own R&D and proprietary technology. Chinese funds usually placed their bet on a particular team rather than on a specific asset. Consequently, backed by venture capitalists, Chinese biopharmas went out on a buying spree to beef up their pipelines. As a result a booming in-licensing business developed where cash rish Chinese biopharma companies started to in-license greater China rights for often later stage clinical stage assets from American and European companies.

In 2017 Chinese companies in-licensed 37 assets or technologies from abroad; a number that grew to 85 in 2019.[16] 2021 saw the peak of this trend with almost 100 in-licensing deals.[17] In general US companies benefited most from this trend. Most Chinese biotech CEOs had worked and lived in the US for a long time, and knew the ecosystem and the market well. For them it was easier to partner with US companies than

---

[16] S&P Global. 2021. Chinese drugmakers look overseas to beef up pipelines with licensing deals. www.spglobal.com/marketintelligence/en/news-insights/latest-news-headlines/chinese-drugmakers-look-overseas-to-beef-up-pipelines-with-licensing-deals-62942864. Accessed on December 9, 2023.

[17] MSQ Ventures. 2021. 2021 China biopharma global transactions and IPOs review. https://msqventures.com/msq-viewpoints/2021-china-biopharma-global-transactions-and-ipos-review-1. Accessed on December 9, 2023.

European ones. The pipelines of most Chinese biotechs—companies like Zai Lab, Everest Medicines and Cstone Pharmaceuticals for instance—were originally completely built around drugs licensed from abroad. When Everest Medicines listed in Hong Kong in 2020, all eight products in its pipeline had been developed externally. Probably the biggest contributor and beneficiary from this trend was multinational pharma, Eli Lilly. Between the period 2015–2019 it out-licensed seven treatments to Chinese drugmakers.[18] This in-licensing trend was also one of the reasons why in 2021 the Chinese NRDL included 2,860 drugs, of which 1,486 were 'Western'-innovated medicines.[19]

But there was also a downsize to this. As value needed to be created rapidly, Chinese licensees often in-licensed assets and technology which were not necessarily first-in-class or best-in-class. Pipelines were getting filled, but not necessarily with the best assets. During those times, money was readily available, and speed prevailed over quality. So traditionally most China-originated biopharmas concentrated on a small pool of derisked mechanisms of action (MoAs) because that's what was easy to develop further in China. At the same time these biotechs were not built as global companies, as the in-licensed assets were only for commercialization in China. This meant that own research had to be brought up to speed and develop real first-in-class assets, in order to transform into a company with global potential.

---

[18] S&P Global. 2021. Chinese drugmakers look overseas to beef up pipelines with licensing deals. www.spglobal.com/marketintelligence/en/news-insights/latest-news-headlines/chinese-drugmakers-look-overseas-to-beef-up-pipelines-with-licensing-deals-62942864. Accessed on December 9, 2023.

[19] Pharma Technology. 2021. China's latest NRDL update continues to exclude foreign PD-1 inhibitors, favours rare disease drugs. https://www.pharmaceutical-technology.com/pricing-and-market-access/china-nrdl-foreign-pd1-inhibitors/?cf-view. Accessed on November 26, 2023.

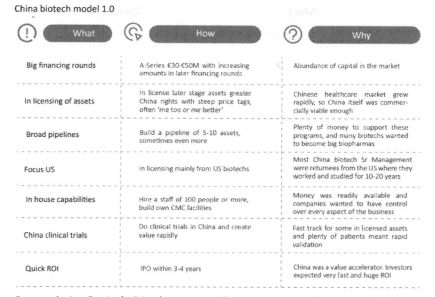

Source Agio Capital, Biopharma in China, a pivot to Europe. 2023

HKEX and STAR Market Opening Up

Another important part of the success story and emergence of the Chinese biopharma sector, was the opening up of the Hong Kong Stock Exchange (HKEX) in 2018 to pre-revenue life sciences companies.[20] Previously China didn't have a NASDAQ style secondary market. This means it was impossible for pre-revenue companies—as nearly all biopharma startup companies are—to pursue a public listing in China or Hong Kong. The opening up of the HKEX was therefore a significant step in providing Chinese biotech firms with more access to capital to fuel R&D.

The Hong Kong Stock Exchange's listing reforms launched in 2018 opened a whole new pathway for pre-revenue biotech companies to raise funds, fuelling an era of growth. While Shanghai continues to be the leading hub for China's biotech industry, the new listing regime—the

---

[20] South China Morning Post. 2021. Three years on from listing reforms, Hong Kong's biotech investment ecosystem is booming. https://www.scmp.com/presented/business/topics/hkex-and-future-biotech/article/3148541/three-years-listing-reforms-hong. Accessed on November 25, 2023.

so-called Chapter 18A—has propelled the Hong Kong Stock Exchange (HKEX) to become a leading capital market for biotech companies. Three years after its launch, Hong Kong had become Asia's largest biotech fundraising hub, and the second-largest globally.[21] Between 2018 and 2022 there has been a surge of interest in biotechnology companies seeking listings in Hong Kong, matched by strong investor appetites to support this sector, which has become one of the fastest-growing IPO market segments. By the end of 2022, 56 companies—all China-originated biotechs—had listed under this biotech regime. 20 of them had their headquarters in Shanghai, ten in Suzhou, nine in Beijing, six in Hangzhou and the rest scattered over other cities in China.[22]

Hong Kong regulators designed the biotech regulatory regime in such a way to ensure that only pre-revenue biotech companies at a relatively advanced stage of development were able to list on HKEX. A company must have at least one core asset which is beyond the concept stage. This means in practice that companies with IPO aspirations must have drugs under development which have entered phase II clinical trials.[23] HKEX also permits companies to rely on an in-licensed product to meet this 'Core Product' requirement, which suits many China-originated biotechs as they engage heavily in licensing activities.

---

[21] South China Morning Post. 2021. Three years on from listing reforms, Hong Kong's biotech investment ecosystem is booming. https://www.scmp.com/presented/business/topics/hkex-and-future-biotech/article/3148541/three-years-listing-reforms-hong. Accessed on November 25, 2023.

[22] Skadden. 2023. Report on Hong Kong-Listed biotech companies. www.skadden.com/-/media/files/publications/2023/04/2023-report-on-hong-kong-listed-biotech-companies/hk_biotech_survey_english.pdf?rev=a72b0aebbdfc45af91b0e9abd6983726&hash=7719790B0890FF3134E0E59FB395E7D5. Accessed on October 29, 2023.

[23] China Business Law Journal. 2022. Chapter 18A listings of biotech companies on the HKEX. https://law.asia/chapter-18a-listings-of-biotech-companies-on-the-hkex/. Accessed on October 29, 2023.

Number of Companies Listed by Year

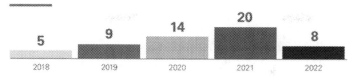

Source Skadden. Report on Hong Kong-listed biotech companies. 2023

In 2019 the Chinese regulators launched the mainland version of NASDAQ. The Shanghai Stock Exchange's Science and Technology Innovation Board, also known as the STAR Market, was established with an aim to help the growing number of China's technology and innovation enterprises to raise funds in the domestic capital market.[24] Unlike the Shanghai and Shenzhen stock exchanges in China, the financial requirements of the STAR Market are less focused on assets, cash flow and net income. Companies in high-tech fields, such as new materials, biomedicine and information technology, are the main targets. By June 2023 20 innovative biopharmaceutical companies had been listed on the STAR Market, raising US$5.9 billion. It also attracted five leading 18A companies listed at the HKEX (Junshi Biosciences, Cansino Biologics, RemeGen, BeiGene and InnoCare Pharma) to return to Shanghai for a dual listing.[25] BeiGene even achieved a unique feat. In 2021 it became the first triple-listed biotech company on NASDAQ, Hong Kong Stock Exchange and STAR Market.[26]

Although at first sight HKEX and the STAR Market look similar, they are notable differences. Just like HKEX, the STAR Market also allows

---

[24] EY, 2022. How does Shanghai's STAR Market support innovation enterprises' IPO. https://www.ey.com/en_cn/china-opportunities/how-does-shanghai-s-star-market-support-innovation-enterprise-s-ipos. Accessed on October 29, 2023.

[25] China Securities Journal. 2023. Listed companies reach 20! http://english.sse.com.cn/news/newsrelease/voice/c/5723142.shtml. Accessed on October 20, 2023.

[26] Beigene. 2021. Beigene announces closing of its RMB22.2 billion (US$3.5 billion) Initial Public Offering on the STAR Market of the Shanghai Stock Exchange.in China. https://ir.beigene.com/news/beigene-announces-closing-of-its-rmb22-2-billion-us-3-5-billion-initial-public-offering-on-the-star/5c078534-a007-4d0b-8d42-bacb7c643f86/. Accessed on November 29, 2023.

the listing of highly innovative biotech companies that are not yet profitable, but the thresholds are higher than listings in Hong Kong. In the STAR Market there is a higher dependence on window guidance -basically following more the policy. Chapter 18A has a more transparent regulatory approval process, allowing for pre-listing consultation and communication with the HKEX. That means going public in Shanghai is more difficult. In 2021 alone, 17 biopharmaceutical companies failed to complete their IPO on the Star Market.[27]

Although for China originated biopharma companies, IPOs have become fairly common now, entering public markets via Special Purpose Acquisition Companies (SPAC) is a rare occasion. SPAC listings have not yet been approved in mainland China, but they are allowed in Hong Kong since January 2022, following a series of reforms aimed at revitalizing the market. Some Chinese biopharmas have successfully done a SPAC listing in the US. In March 2023 YS Biopharma went public in Nasdaq through a merger with Summit Healthcare Acquisition Corporation, a SPAC. Also, the same year Apollomics was listed on Nasdaq through a SPAC merger with Maxpro Capital Acquisition Corporation.[28]

Many Chinese biopharma companies have greatly benefited from the new listing regulations.

The market value of China originated, publicly listed innovative life sciences companies across the Nasdaq, HKEX, and STAR Market surged from US$ 3 billion in 2016 to more than US$ 380 billion in July 2021. Within that amount, the market capitalization of Chinese biopharma companies grew from US$ 1 billion in 2016 to over US$ 180 billion in 2021.[29]

---

[27] China Business Law Journal. 2022. Chapter 18A listings of biotech companies on the HKEX. https://law.asia/chapter-18a-listings-of-biotech-companies-on-the-hkex/. Accessed on October 29, 2023.

[28] Bioworld. 2023. China's biopharma firms need enough cash to get through 'capital winter'. https://www.bioworld.com/articles/697643-chinas-biopharma-firms-need-enough-cash-to-get-through-capital-winter?v=preview. Accessed on November 5, 2023.

[29] McKinsey & Co. 2021. The dawn of China biopharma innovation. https://www.mckinsey.com/industries/life-sciences/our-insights/the-dawn-of-china-biopharma-innovation. Accessed on November 15, 2023.

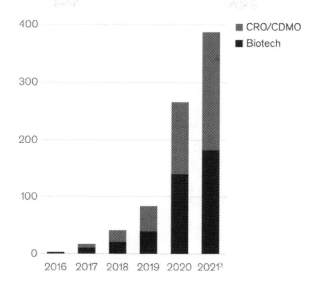

Source McKinsey & Co. 2021. The dawn of China biopharma innovation

Between 2016 and 2021 the speed of public listings accelerated. 2020 was the peak year with 23 IPOs. Chinese biotechs were leading in IPO fundraising as seven out of the world's top 20 largest biopharma IPOs from 2018 to 2020 originated from China.[30]

---

[30] McKinsey & Co. 2021. The dawn of China biopharma innovation. https://www.mckinsey.com/industries/life-sciences/our-insights/the-dawn-of-china-biopharma-innovation. Accessed on November 15, 2023.

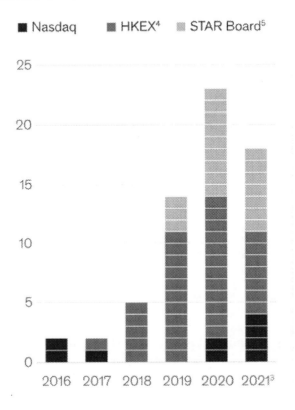

Source McKinsey & Co. 2021. The dawn of China biopharma innovation

The rising share value of the MSCI China Health Care Index, which captures large and mid-cap representation across China H shares, B shares, Red chips and P chips, also shows how the biopharma sector fueled this growth.[31] It was only after venture capital poured into the biopharma sector, and the consequent public listings of new biopharma companies that the MSCI China Health Care Index started to go up rapidly.

---

[31] MSCI China Health Care Index (HKD). 2023. Index Factsheet. www.msci.com/documents/10199/53d45d8e-28a9-4a1f-8f91-c9dfddaf10bc. Accessed on November 29, 2023.

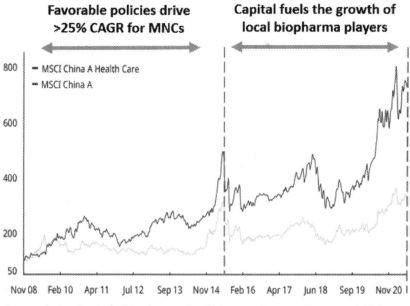

Source Agio Capital, Biopharma in China, a pivot to Europe. 2023

Despite these past impressive numbers, Hong Kong and China's healthcare cap is still underdeveloped compared to the US market. In 2020 the total US market capitalization for healthcare companies was around US$5.5 trillion (that is all biotech, major pharma, specialty pharma, medtech and services combined) while the total China healthcare market cap in the same year was around US$ 1.5 trillion (US$400 billion of HKEX listings plus US$ 1 trillion of China domestic listings). The development of a true financial biotech market in Hong Kong and China will take time. IPOs slowed down significantly since late 2021, and a reopening of the IPO window is unlikely before 2025. Hong Kong still sees its share of biotech IPOs but due to deteriorating market conditions the amount of public listings in 2002 decreased for the first time since 2018. During 2022, only eight biotech companies listed on HKEX, raised an average of US$59 million, which is a significant reduction compared to 2021 when the average money raised was US$243 million, or US$345 million in 2020.[32]

There will be more setbacks, but many elements of the ecosystem are in place to ensure long-term growth. Especially the HKEX listings have helped facilitate the opening up of China's biotech sector to venture capital and partnerships with international companies. These IPOs give global investors the opportunity to look at innovations coming out of the Chinese biotech sector.[33]

Biotech Parks Have Mushroomed

As all these biopharma companies needed a place to locate, the Chinese government supported the development of science parks and city hubs to attract and cluster innovation and R&D. Authorities offered land to developers on attractive terms to develop R&D parks. According to the Boston Consulting Group—depending on the definition—the number of biotech science parks grew from about 400 to about 600 between 2016 and 2020.[34] Gradually bio clusters were being created in China, similar to those in Europe like Lyon in France, the Flanders region in Belgium, Oxford and Cambridge in the UK, or Massachusetts and California in the US. The aim of these clusters is to build new biopharma ecosystems and facilitate collaboration between academia, education and industry. The Chinese government has established seven biomedical city clusters. Most well-known are the Jing-Jin-Ji area (Beijing, Tianjin, Hebei), the Yangtze River Delta (Shanghai, Suzhou, Wuxi, Hangzhou) and the Greater Bay Area (Shenzhen, Guangzhou), and cities like Chengdu or

---

[32] Skadden. 2023. Report on Hong Kong-Listed biotech companies. www.skadden.com/-/media/files/publications/2023/04/2023-report-on-hong-kong-listed-biotech-companies/hk_biotech_survey_english.pdf?rev=a72b0aebbdfc45af91b0e9abd6983726&hash=7719790B0890FF3134E0E59FB395E7D5. Accessed on October 29, 2023.

[33] South China Morning Post. 2021. Three years on from listing reforms, Hong Kong's biotech investment ecosystem is booming. https://www.scmp.com/presented/business/topics/hkex-and-future-biotech/article/3148541/three-years-listing-reforms-hong. Accessed on November 25, 2023.

[34] Boston Consulting Group. 2020 Competing in China's booming biopharma market. https://www.bcg.com/publications/2020/competing-in-chinas-biopharma-market. Accessed on September 8, 2023.

Wuhan in central and western China.[35] These regions host industrial zones that incubate key research entities and companies that facilitate technical development. There are countless examples, and some do better than others. Notably good examples of thriving activity are the Shanghai Zhangjiang High-Tech Park (Zhangjiang Pharma Valley), Suzhou, in Jiangsu province, which is home to BioBAY industrial park and Xi'an Jiaotong-Liverpool University, and Guangzhou Bio-Island.[36] All these locations host a considerable number of the world's top pharmaceutical companies, such as Novartis, Roche, Pfizer and AstraZeneca, including their R&D center. At the same time nearly all Chinese pharma companies and most notable biotech companies have set up shop there also, together with CROs, CDMOs, incubation centers and so forth. All these locations are hotbeds of innovation and enjoy a thriving ecosystem.

This model makes of course perfectly sense and is an inevitable must-have if China wants to create truly home-grown, self-sufficient talent and innovation. One notable difference with US or European science parks, however, is that—as so many initiatives in China—the setup in China is more aspirational and top-down driven and feels less organic and more forced than its US and European examples.[37] But the model definitely has its benefits, as has been proven to work successfully.

---

[35] China Briefing. 2022. China's biopharma industry: market prospects, investment paths. https://www.china-briefing.com/news/china-booming-biopharmaceuticals-market-innovation-investment-opportunities/. Accessed on November 15, 2023.

[36] Pharmaceutical Executive. 2022. China invests in building biotech. www.pharmexec.com/view/china-invests-in-building-biotech. Accessed on September 9, 2023.

[37] Pharmaceutical Executive. 2022. China invests in building biotech. www.pharmexec.com/view/china-invests-in-building-biotech. Accessed on September 9, 2023.

Name	Province/Municipality	City
Shanghai Zhangjiang Medicine Valley	Shanghai	Shanghai
Suzhou BioBAY	Jiangsu	Suzhou
Zhongguancun Life Science Park	Beijing	Beijing
Beijing Yizhuang Biomedical Park	Beijing	Beijing
Wuhan BioLake	Hubei	Wuhan
Guangzhou Science City Bio Industry Park	Guangdong	Guangzhou
ELHT Hangzhou Biomedical Industrial Park	Zhejiang	Hangzhou
Chengdu Hi-Tech Industrial Development Zone	Sichuan	Chengdu
Nanjing Biotech and Pharmaceutical Valley	Jiangsu	Nanjing
China Medical City	Jiangsu	Taizhou

Source Deloitte. 2021. China's biotech parks—leveraging the ecosystem for success

Set up in 2006 Suzhou bioBAY is the biggest biotech park in China, closely followed by Zhangjiang High-Tech Park in Shanghai. BioBAY is home to 630 companies, of which 24 are listed ones. 22 biotechs have already marketed drugs also. On the 2020 competitiveness ranking of Chinese biomedical industry clusters released by the Ministry of Science and Technology (MOST) of China, BioBAY ranked first in terms of comprehensive competitiveness, industrial competitiveness, talent competitiveness and technological competitiveness[38].

---

[38] bioBAY. 2023. About BioBAY. https://www.biobay.com.cn/en/about/introduction. Accessed on November 26, 2023.

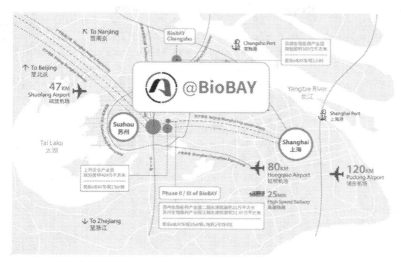

Source Atlatl. 2023. Location

GLOBALLY INTEGRATED AND COMPETITIVE CRO/CMO INDUSTRY

Unsurprisingly for a country which is known as the factory of the world, manufacturing is a very crucial part of its development. China's biopharma sector is no different. Its CROs and CDMOs are an important part of the pharma space and have grown rapidly fueled by venture capitalists and the demands of the market. Compared to the US or Europe Chinese CROs started off later. Originated in the US in the 1970s, CROs expanded rapidly in 1980s in the US, Europe and Japan, and evolved in mature companies in the late 1990s. China however did not see the first CRO until 1996, when the US company MDS Pharmaceutical Services, entered the market. China's local CROs started to emerge at the beginning of the twenty-first century. A whole new breed of Chinese domestic CROs popped up and developed fast since China started in 2003 to permit clinical trial sponsors to entrust trial-related tasks to CROs.[39]

---

[39] National Library of Medicine. 2014. Contract Research Organizations (CRO) in China: integrating Chinese research and development capabilities for global drug innovation. www.ncbi.nlm.nih.gov/pmc/articles/PMC4240890/. Accessed on November 2, 2023.

Fast forward to 2023, an emerging pharmaceutical sector and billions of dollars of investment later, China has developed a tremendous and state-of-the-art vibrant ecosystem of contract research organizations (CROs), contract development and manufacturing organizations (CDMOs) and other service providers. China's CRO market reached almost US$ 10 billion in 2021, taking up 13.2% of the global market.[40]

China has now built a globally competitive CRO/CDMO industry with global footprints, quality, speed and efficiency. Two out of the ten global pre-clinical CROs, one of the global clinical CRO and three of the top ten global CDMO/CMO are China-originated companies. The Chinese CROs and CDMOS not only provide very reliable quality, but they are also very cost-efficient with economies of scale. And as so many other companies in China, they are also very agile in their operations. Chinese CROs are as developed as their multinational peers, such as IQVIA, LabCorp and ICON. In 2022 three China-based CROs—Wuxi AppTec, Pharmaron and AsymChem—are globally ranked among the top ten CROs in terms of revenue. In 2021 these three received more than three-quarters of their revenues from non-China customers. Much of their revenue comes from MNCs highlighting the fact that they are able to attract international clients[41]. Wuxi Apptec, established in 2000, is China's best performing company and ranked fifth in the world in terms of revenue.[42] In 2022 its global revenue was US$ 5.6 billion of which 81% outside China. Wuxi Apptec has also labs, manufacturing sites and offices in nine countries.

Not only have Chinese CROs and CDMOs become global players, but in some fields Chinese CROs are becoming world leaders. WuXi AppTec and Pharmaron for instance are now the world's largest providers

---

[40] Baipharm. 2022. China contract research organization (CRO) industry 2022 review. https://baipharm.chemlinked.com/news/china-contract-research-organizat ion-cro-2022-review-and-outlook. Accessed on November 19, 2023.

[41] McKinsey & Co. 2022. Vision 2028: How China could impact the global biopharma industry. https://www.mckinsey.com/~/media/mckinsey/industries/life%20sciences/our%20insights/vision%202028%20how%20china%20could%20impact%20the%20global%20biopharma%20industry/vision-2028-how-china-could-impact-the-global-biopharma-industry.a#:~:text=Biopharmas%20originating%20in%20China%20will,determine%20how%20the%20industry%20grows. Accessed on November 19, 2023.

[42] Baipharm. 2022. China contract research organization (CRO) industry 2022 review. https://baipharm.chemlinked.com/news/china-contract-research-organizat ion-cro-2022-review-and-outlook. Accessed on November 19, 2023.

of preclinical chemistry services.[43] Other CROs and CDMOs are also expanding globally. CRO dMed merged with Clinipace, a US-based CRO,[44] while one of China's biggest CDMO Chime Biologics is actively looking to expand to Europe. Small-and-medium-sized Chinese CROs on the other hand are often not so developed in their research capabilities. Some provide regulatory affair services only.

In the manufacturing space, Chinese CDMOs are also extending their services into biologics, despite the fact that homegrown biotechs have begun to develop their own capability and capacity of independent biologics to secure quality and supply. Set up in 2015, CDMO WuXi Biologics is now in the top five companies in terms of manufacturing capacity for biologics.[45] China's top CDMOs and biotechs now account for about 7% of the world's monoclonal antibody (mAb) capacity. China has now also proved itself to be a high quality, cost-competitive manufacturing hub for small molecules, producing active pharmaceutical ingredients (APIs) and generics that regularly secure approval from the FDA and the EMEA.[46]

Clinical Trials Are Skyrocketing

The mushrooming of CROs and the explosive developments in the biopharma sector resulted in a skyrocketing number of clinical trials being conducted in China. Spurred on by all these investment, the number of innovative assets under clinical development in China has tripled between

---

[43] McKinsey & C0. 2021. The dawn of China biopharma innovation. www.mckinsey.com/industries/life-sciences/our-insights/the-dawn-of-china-biopharma-innovation. Accessed on November 19, 2023.

[44] Caidya. 2022. CROs dMed and Clinipace merge to accelerate customer success. www.caidya.com/news/cros-dmed-and-clinipace-merge-to-accelerate-customer-success/. Accessed on November 19, 2023.

[45] Pharmaphorum. 2023. FDA's treatment of China developed drugs spurs demand for multiregional clinical trials. https://pharmaphorum.com/market-access-2/fdas-treatment-of-china-developed-drugs-spurs-demands. Accessed on November 18, 2023.

[46] McKinsey & Co. 2022. Vision 2028: How China could impact the global biopharma industry. https://www.mckinsey.com/~/media/mckinsey/industries/life%20sciences/our%20insights/vision%202028%20how%20china%20could%20impact%20the%20global%20biopharma%20industry/vision-2028-how-china-could-impact-the-global-biopharma-industry.a#:~:text=Biopharmas%20originating%20in%20China%20will,determine%20how%20the%20industry%20grows. Accessed on November 19, 2023.

2017 and 2022. And most of them came from China. In 2022 almost 80% of the 1,760 assets under clinical development came from Chinese biopharmas.

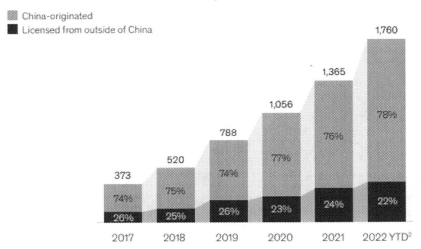

Source McKinsey & Co. 2022. Vision 2028: How China could impact the global biopharma industry

One of the reasons why so many trials are being done in China is related to the speed advantages of China. The leading Chinese biotechs spend 12 to 20 months from target validation to PCC. This is 30 to 50% faster than the industry average, which is about 24 to 36 months. This means that Chinese companies can harness the discovery, trial execution efficiency and speed of the Chinese healthcare ecosystem.

When looking at the clinical development stage, broadly speaking 50% of all industry sponsored clinical trials in China are in Phase I, 20% in Phase II and Phase III, and around 10% in Phase IV. This means that China is a place where early-stage innovation is being done.

Industry sponsored studies by trial phase in China

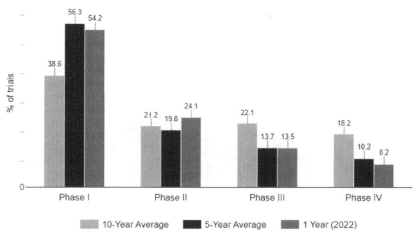

Source Clinical Trials Arena. 2023. China accounts for 27.7% share of global clinical trial activity in 2022

In terms of what therapeutics field is most interesting, the figures from 2022 show that for industry sponsored clinical trials in China, 35% of the trials were conducted in oncology. Infectious disease and central nervous system both held around 12% share. Cardiovascular held an 9% and metabolic disorders held an 8.6% share, over a five-year average of 9.8% and a ten-year average of 9.8%.

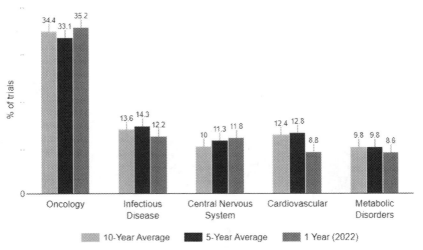

Source Clinical Trials Arena. 2023. China accounts for 27.7% share of global clinical trial activity in 2022

The Chinese Biopharma Sector Has Come of Age

After a decade of expansion, the Chinese biopharma sector has established itself as a sector which is here to stay. China biopharma went through a tremendous growth phase before 2021, with many companies created and funds raised, formation of an innovation ecosystem, and value chain capability build-up with scaled fast-following innovations. Today the four leading bio clusters are home of 8.500 biotech companies, most of them set up during the hype between 2018 and 2022.[47] At the 2023 China Healthcare Summit, McKinsey said more than 30,000 job opportunities were added by the top ten listed biotechs. Moreover, every year more than 500 Investigational New Drug Applications (IND) are initiated by China originated biopharma companies. The GDP impact of the biopharma sector, however, still remains limited, as most companies are not yet making profit. McKinsey calculated that with its size of US$20 billion,

---

[47] Harri Jarvelainen. 2023. Key takeaways from the McKinsey China Biopharma report 2023—Growing pains and more. https://www.linkedin.com/pulse/key-takeaways-from-mckinsey-china-biopharma-report-harri-3rf3c. Accessed on November 22, 2023.

the Chinese biopharma sector is only tiny compared to the US biopharma market, which is worth US$415 billion. The Chinese biopharma sector only contributes 3% to the global biopharma market. This is very low compared to the market of consumer goods (20%) or cars (30%) for which China is the biggest market. This, however, also means there is room for growth. McKinsey estimates that the biopharma market in China will grow to US$ 50 billion in 2028, hence adding US$30 billion in six years' time.

Innovation in the Chinese Biopharma Sector: From Me-too to First-in-Class

Abstract China is moving from 'Made in China' to 'Designed in China'. In the biopharma space this is no different. China's biotech innovation is really only a decade old, but a momentous shift has occurred already. By now China's R&D has come a long way, moving away from generic drugs to the latest technologies. Starting in the early 2000s, a first wave of new generation innovative pharma companies formed in China. As scientific research and core R&D however was not at a level to produce first-in-class innovation, these companies aimed on being fast followers for me-too and me-better drugs. Around 2016, the Chinese biopharma landscape started to evolve again, and a next wave of innovation emerged. Chinese companies started to deepen its scientific understanding and started to work on novel biotechnologies. While not being first-in-class, companies embarked on more innovation, especially in the field of antibodies. Learning from past experiences and urged on by their investors, since 2020 an increasing number of Chinese biopharmas have embarked on a strategy to develop first-in-class drugs with global potential using novel technologies. Especially during the pandemic, China became host to a fleet of new biotech firms that raked in enormous amounts of funding during the height of the venture capital boom. Many companies are now working in the gene and cell therapy field, RNA-related technologies, radiopharmaceutical drugs and all kinds of new cutting-edge technologies. By far the most promising way how China could leapfrog in drug discovery and overcome traditional problems, is applying Artificial Intelligence (AI) to the process.

© The Author(s), under exclusive license to Springer Nature Singapore Pte Ltd. 2024
S. Agten and B. Wu, *Biopharma in China*,
https://doi.org/10.1007/978-981-97-1471-1_4

The results of all this are increasingly visible. Where Chinese biopharma companies traditionally in-licensed new assets from abroad, in 2023 there was more out-licensing than in-licensing activity. The innovation potential of China is now unquestioned. Given the fact that the Chinese biopharma sector only exists for not yet a decade, this is a remarkable achievement. But despite having great strides going forward, Chinese biopharma has yet to produce a substantial number of patented drugs that can compete globally and commercialized around the world, and challenges remain.

Keywords Antibody · AI-driven drug discovery (AIDD) · Best-in-class and First-in-class · CAR-T · Clinical trials · In-licensing · Out-licensing · Me-too, me-better strategy · Mechanism of action (MoA) · RNA

As well documented by now, China is moving from 'Made in China' to 'Designed in China'. In the biopharma space this is no different. China's biotech innovation is really only a decade old, but a momentous shift has occurred already. Where local Chinese companies used to be generic players, innovation was in the hands of the MNCs. Over the years local companies started their innovation process and added new R&D to the mix. Most recently this Chinese innovation is moving overseas as Chinese biopharma companies have started to develop some first-in-class drugs with global potential.

China's R&D has come a long way and the evolution of China's biggest biotech park, BioBAY Suzhou, sums up this journey well. BioBAY was initiated in 2006 when it started to attract scientists from home and abroad, with an expertise mostly in small molecule drugs, and generic drugs. From the year 2011 BioBAY started to look at projects of biosimilars, and for the next ten years, BioBAY focused all its resources into the up-stream, pilot-run and down-stream capabilities. By the year 2018, the park started to look at new modalities like gene therapy, cell therapy and nuclear-acid, siRNA and mRNA drugs. This captures well the journey of most biopharma companies, from generic drugs to the latest technologies.

Innovation Wave 1.0: Me-too, Me-Better Strategy

Starting in the early 2000s, a first wave of new generation innovative pharma companies was formed in China. As mentioned before the strategy of most biopharma companies was two-fold. On the one hand, they embarked on in-licensing from abroad in order to get innovative drugs on the market rapidly. On the other hand, they would start their own research and development activities. But as scientific research and core R&D were not at a level to produce first-in-class innovation, these companies aimed on being fast followers for me-too and me-better drugs. They sought new molecules on validated or late-stage clinical targets or combination therapies.[1] This so-called 'Me-too, me-better' strategy utilized the Chinese healthcare ecosystem of hospitals and service providers, to provide low-cost alternatives to first-in-class drugs. Most Chinese biopharmas concentrated on a small pool of de-risked mechanisms of action (MoA) because that's what was in their pipelines.[2] These companies also pursued a 'China for China' innovation strategy. Not only was their home market poised to grow, but these companies also knew they lacked the scientific, commercial and organizational capabilities to harvest global ambitions.

Companies like Hutchison China MediTech (founded in 2000), BeiGene (founded in 2010), Innovent Biologics and Hua Medicine (both founded in 2011) and Junshi Biosciences (founded in 2012) are now household names but were in fact all set up during this first wave of innovation.[3] Unlike the more therapeutically diverse research landscape in Europe or the US, oncology was the dominant theme among Chinese biotechs of the first wave. Some cardiovascular and metabolic diseases are very prevalent in China but failed to attract attention from domestic firms. Their focus was on oncology as China has a large cancer population that was often underserved. BeiGene was a prime example. From the

---

[1] BCG. 2020. Competing in China's booming biopharma market. www.bcg.com/publications/2020/competing-in-chinas-biopharma-market. Accessed on November 22, 2023.

[2] McKinsey & Co. 2022. Vision 2028: How China could impact the global biopharma industry. https://www.mckinsey.com/~/media/mckinsey/industries/life%20sciences/our%20insights/vision%202028%20how%20china%20could%20impact%20the%20global%20biopharma%20industry/vision-2028-how-china-could-impact-the-global-biopharma-industry.pdf. Accessed on October 28, 2023.

[3] FiercePharma. 2020. 10 biotechs to know in China. https://www.fiercepharma.com/special-report/10-biotechs-to-know-china. Accessed on November 22, 2023.

get-go, the goal was to build China's Genentech, focused on cancer, especially types that affect Chinese people.[4] Innovent Biologics embarked on the same route with its self-proclaimed mission 'to develop, manufacture and commercialize high-quality innovative medicines for the treatment of cancer and other major diseases'.[5]

The 'Me too, me better' strategy was being reflected in the pipelines of many Chinese biopharma companies, as they mainly focused on continual development and incremental innovation. And as always in China there was fierce competition. As most companies were all pursuing the same targets, China became a notoriously overcrowded market for some targets. This was specifically so for anticancer PD-1 inhibitor drugs, as they had been included on the NRDL list. In 2018 25 Chinese PD-1/PD-L1 inhibitors submitted a registration application in China.[6] Two years later more than 50 Chinese companies were focused on PD-1/PD-L1 candidates, looking for improved efficacy, safety, and convenience.[7] China's domestic pharma companies mainly relied on copying the development of leading antibodies in the global market. That is, generating mouse antibodies through hybridoma and then humanizing the lead candidates. As this innovation wave continued, the focus shifted more from 'me-too' toward 'me-better' innovations. This kind of 'affordable innovation' became very standard in China. Only a few biotechs focused on unique indications to make their molecules stand out.

The first wave of innovation not only produced fierce competition for the same targets, but also dramatically reduced the time between global first-in-class assets and fast followers. The timeline gap was closed because Chinese biopharma companies took on more risk by developing compounds earlier in order to follow the first-in-class players more quickly. China's pharma companies can also execute trials faster, thanks

---

[4] FiercePharma. 2020. 10 biotechs to know in China. https://www.fiercepharma.com/special-report/10-biotechs-to-know-china. Accessed on November 22, 2023.

[5] Innovent Bio. 2023. Company overview. https://www.innoventbio.com/AboutUs/CompanyOverview. Accessed on November 22, 2023.

[6] PharmaExec. 2018. The PD-/PD-L1 race in China. https://www.pharmexec.com/view/pd-1-pd-l1-race-china. Accessed on November 22, 2023.

[7] FiercePharma. 2020. 10 biotechs to know in China. https://www.fiercepharma.com/special-report/10-biotechs-to-know-china. Accessed on November 22, 2023.

to the size and increasing maturity of the clinical sites in China.[8] As a result, this strategy started to bear fruit. In 2015 the total number of first-time clinical trial applications from domestic companies for a new drug was 79 for small-molecule drugs and 20 for therapeutic biologics. Of the seven new molecules approved in China in 2016, three were developed by domestic firms. In 2018 and 2019, Chinese biopharmas contributed 14 and 13 new drug approvals in the country, respectively.[9]

Unsurprisingly the first wave of homegrown Chinese innovative drugs with global potential revolved nearly all around PD-1/PD-L1 antibodies. Despite Europe and the US leading this field and acquiring vast experience and knowledge over the years, Chinese pharma companies Hengrui, Beigene, Zai Lab, Innovent Biologics and Junshi Biosciences entered the Chinese market with commercialized new drugs. In 2018, BMS and Merck successfully received approvals for their PD-1 antibodies in China, becoming the first two players there. Junshi Pharma and Innovent Bio, however, snatched greenlights from the NMPA within less than half a year. Soon after, Hengrui Medicine became the third domestic pharma granted approval.[10]

In 2020 there were already eight PD-1/L1 agents on the market, with more to follow.[11] It's this first wave of homegrown innovation which resulted in a milestone in 2021 when local drug approvals surpassed those of MNCs. Since 2018 more than 100 China-originated innovative drugs have been approved in China.

[8] BCG. 2020. Competing in China's booming biopharma market. www.bcg.com/publications/2020/competing-in-chinas-biopharma-market. Accessed on November 22, 2023.

[9] FiercePharma. 2020. 10 biotechs to know in China. https://www.fiercepharma.com/special-report/10-biotechs-to-know-china. Accessed on November 22, 2023.

[10] PharmaExec. 2019. The PD-1 race in China heats up. https://www.pharmexec.com/view/pd-1-race-china-heats. Accessed on October 26, 2023.

[11] FiercePharma. 2020. 10 biotechs to know in China. https://www.fiercepharma.com/special-report/10-biotechs-to-know-china. Accessed on November 22, 2023.

Local drug approvals bypassed those of multinational corporations (MNCs) in 2021 and began to generate sizable revenue.

NDA approvals for innovative drugs, 2017–21

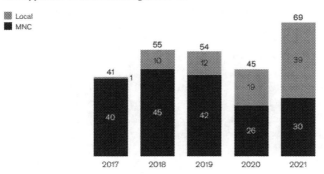

Source McKinsey, Vision 2028. How China could impact the global biopharma industry. 2022

In total in the decade between 2011 and 2021, the NMPA approved 353 new drugs, 220 small molecules, 86 biologics and 47 vaccines. The approval of 70 new drugs in 2021 was a record high.[12]

Innovation Wave 2.0: Innovation on Innovation

Beginning around 2016, the Chinese biopharma landscape started to evolve, and a next wave of innovation emerged. As Chinese companies started to deepen its understanding in areas such as oncology pathogenesis, biological mechanisms and antibody engineering, there was more activity in original indication expansion, combo therapies and novel antibodies (such as bispecific, fusion proteins and ADC). While not being first-in-class, these areas demand not only more risk taking than simply being a fast follower, but also requires more innovation expertise, from hypothesis to clinical translation.[13] It was also around that period that a new generation of Chinese biopharma companies were being established.

---

[12] National Library of Medicine. 2023. Trends and characteristics of new drug approvals in China, 2011–2021. www.ncbi.nlm.nih.gov/pmc/articles/PMC9628473/. Accessed on November 26, 2023.

[13] BCG. 2020. Competing in China's booming biopharma market. www.bcg.com/publications/2020/competing-in-chinas-biopharma-market. Accessed on November 22, 2023.

Zai Lab was established in 2013, Cstone Pharmaceuticals in 2015, I-Mab Biopharma and Harbour Biomed in 2016, to name a few.[14]

Many of these companies of the second wave explored novel antibodies, particularly bispecific antibodies. Their innovation on bispecific antibodies was not limited to new combinations of targets but included platform technologies crucial to the success of bispecifics. Among biopharmas pursuing bispecific monoclonal antibodies in China, some developed original technologies to improve the function, stability and safety of bispecific antibodies. They also developed some original indication expansions in oncology. Chinese pharma companies started to explore three original PD-1 indication expansions in areas with high unmet needs such as nasopharyngeal carcinoma, advanced HCC, and advanced esophageal squamous cell carcinoma. Another novelty was that companies started to explore biologics combos, just like the rest of the world. The difference was that local pharma focused more on combos with mature MoAs that include more than one targeted therapy and usually chemo.[15]

Especially in the ADC field, China has taken the lead in drug development. ADC drug development by itself is nothing new. Early-stage ADC research dates already back to the 1960s, while the first ADC entered clinical trials in the 1980s.[16] But after decades of trial and error in ADC development, the field is poised to deliver a whole new range of targeted drugs to treat a wide range of tumor types and have the potential to be a game changer in revolutionizing cancer treatment. Their development, however, has been challenged by several factors. One key challenge has been the complex nature of ADC design, which requires the combination of a cytotoxic drug, an antibody, a linker and the conjugation technology that connects the components, where each of these components must be optimized depending on the cancer types or targets. Consequently, it can

---

[14] FiercePharma. 2020. 10 biotechs to know in China. https://www.fiercepharma.com/special-report/10-biotechs-to-know-china. Accessed on November 22, 2023.

[15] BCG. 2020. Competing in China's booming biopharma market. www.bcg.com/publications/2020/competing-in-chinas-biopharma-market. Accessed on November 22, 2023.

[16] Single Use Support. 2023. History & development of ADC. https://www.susupport.com/knowledge/bioconjugates/history-development-adcs. Accessed on October 26, 2023.

take years to develop an ADC with the desired therapeutic profile.[17] In 2023 China was ranked as second in the world for ADC development with more than 120 assets under development compared to more than 190 in the US.[18] This might be surprising as only in 2020 the first ADC drug was approved in China,[19] while the FDA already approved the first ADC drug in the US in 2000. But as China has a large population of cancer patients and a growing demand for innovative cancer treatments, it's no surprise that it has become a fertile ground for emerging ADC companies.

Besides antibodies, the competition around peptides also heated up. According to McKinsey, in 2023 there were 43 GLP-1s under development in China.[20] Now in effect the GLP-1 field is at risk of becoming the next PD-1.

Wanting to move away from all this competition, gradually however China's biopharma companies started to work also on novel modalities. Gene and cell editing started to become a focus area. A little-known fact is that the world's first approved gene therapy actually came from a Chinese company, Sibiono GeneTech, already in 2003.[21] and it was the US and Europe which pushed the frontier of scientific discovery in this field. But thanks to a supportive regulatory environment for investigator-initiated trials, China suddenly had the potential again to leapfrog other countries. China has for instance been actively conducting clinical trials with the gene-editing technology CRISPR (clustered regularly interspaced short palindromic repeats) and seized in 2020 the headlines by

[17] Outsourced Pharma. 2023. The ADC market to triple by 2030, driven by big pharma developments. https://www.outsourcedpharma.com/doc/the-adc-market-to-triple-by-driven-by-big-pharma-developments-0001. Accessed on October 26, 2023.

[18] MSQ Ventures. 2023. Global ADC drug development & China opportunities. https://msqventures.com/global-adc-drug-development-china-opportunities-report. Accessed on October 26, 2023.

[19] Xinhuanet, 2020. China introduces expert consensus on ADC drug use. https://www.xinhuanet.com/english/2020-12/05/c_139566078.htm. Accessed on October 26, 2023.

[20] Harri Jarvelainen. 2023. Key takeaways from the McKinsey China Biopharma report 2023—Growing pains and more. https://www.linkedin.com/pulse/key-takeaways-from-mckinsey-china-biopharma-report-harri-3rf3c. Accessed on November 22, 2023.

[21] ePharma. 2020. 10 biotechs to know in China. https://www.fiercepharma.com/special-report/10-biotechs-to-know-china. Accessed on November 22, 2023.

leading the application in human trials.[22] China aims to become a global leader in the field. By mid-2023 for instance the amount of financing in the gene therapy field in China exceeded US$3.3 billion.[23] Well-known companies in the space are Cellular Biomedicine Group[24] and Legend Biotech, both established in 2014.[25] Some companies were set up in collaboration with Western industry leaders. JW Therapeutics—a joint venture between US CAR-T frontrunner Juno Therapeutics and Chinese biopharma manufacturing giant WuXi AppTec—was set up in 2016. Fosun Pharma and Kite Pharma—now a part of Gilead Sciences and another CAR-T pioneer—established Fosun Kite Biotechnology in 2017.[26]

INNOVATION WAVE 3.0: NEW MOAs AND NOVEL TECHNOLOGIES

Learning from past experiences and urged on by their investors, an increasing number of Chinese biopharmas have embarked on a strategy to develop first-in-class drugs with global potential. For most companies these are undoubtedly unchartered waters, but external circumstances forced them to pursue this strategy. The government's strict price restrictions have significantly squeezed drug profit margins, which has forced innovative drug companies to speed up the pace of going international. And that often can only be done by developing really first-in-class assets. Most biotechs established after 2020 are working on first-in-class assets, using novel technologies. Especially during the pandemic China became

---

[22] BCG. 2020. Competing in China's booming biopharma market. www.bcg.com/publications/2020/competing-in-chinas-biopharma-market. Accessed on November 22, 2023.

[23] Labiotech. 2023. Genetic engineering giants: Is China poised to lead the way? https://www.labiotech.eu/in-depth/genetic-engineering-china/. Accessed on November 26, 2023.

[24] Evaluate. 2023, The quiet resurgence of Cellular Biomedicine. https://www.evaluate.com/vantage/articles/news/deals/quiet-resurgence-cellular-biomedicine. Accessed om November 26.

[25] Legend Biotech. 2023. About. https://legendbiotech.com/about/. Accessed on November 26, 2023.

[26] Pharma Boardroom. 2020. Four cell & gene therapy companies to know in China. https://pharmaboardroom.com/articles/four-cell-gene-companies-to-know-in-china/. Accessed on November 26, 2023.

host to a fleet of new biotech firms that raked in enormous amounts of funding during the height of the venture capital boom.

This most recent and advanced level of innovation activities has focused especially on the RNA field. Founded in 2016, Stemirna was in the vanguard of China's mRNA research industry and a pioneering researcher into mRNA,[27] raising in total US$243 million.[28] Following the mRNA hype during the pandemic however, new companies in this field mushroomed, all aiming to develop a mRNA vaccine. Most notable was Abogen which raised a whopping total of US$1.3 billion in funding.[29] Other emerging players in the RNA field are METiS Therapeutics, Rona Therapeutics and Ribo Lifesciences. Therorna from its side, founded in 2021 is a forerunner in circRNA development.[30] In the PROTAC space companies like Hinova and Lynk Pharmaceuticals started to emerge, while in the area of radiopharmaceuticals—radioactive drugs which can be used for the diagnosis and increasingly, for the therapy of diseases—China is also making headways. Sinotau or Full-Life Technologies—with office in Belgium[31]—is forerunners in this field, and more or less head on competing with their Western competitors.

Despite all the advancements made however, it's also clear that Chinese biopharmas are still lagging behind in most areas. A range of new Chinese platform companies have positioned themselves to work in different modalities, but only a small portion of Chinese players are pursuing unique MoA. That means it's still early days for China-originated technology start-ups in the drug R&D space. Some companies in China are making strides and could end up on the forefront of technology-enabled

---

[27] Bambooworks. 2023. China's mRNA pioneer Stemirna faces post-covid reinvention test. https://thebambooworks.com/chinas-mrna-pioneer-stemirna-faces-post-covid-reinvention-test/. Accessed on November 26, 2023.

[28] Dealroom. 2023. Stemirna Therapeutics. https://app.dealroom.co/companies/stemirna_therapeutics. Accessed on November 26, 2023.

[29] Tracxn. 2023. Abogen Biosciences. https://tracxn.com/d/companies/abogen-biosciences/__G_Lnr_ftMDk6heR-tjNDQ-oaAF6EB7HwN1zQiBZ2Dwk. Accessed on November 26, 2023.

[30] Therorna. 2023. Who we are. https://www.therorna.com/about.html. Accessed on November 26, 2023.

[31] Endpoints News. 2023. Sequoia China leads $37 M infusion into radiopharmaceuticals player setting up shop in China and Belgium. https://endpts.com/sequoia-china-leads-37m-infusion-into-radiopharmaceuticals-player-setting-up-shop-in-china-and-belgium/. Accessed on November 26, 2023.

drug discovery and development. AI drug development, cell and gene therapy, radiopharmaceuticals and mRNA show particular promise.

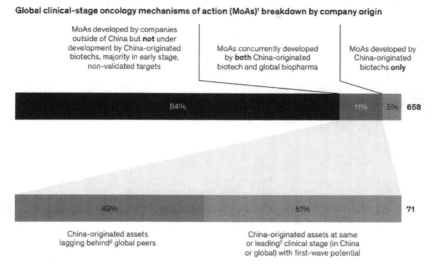

Source McKinsey, Vision 2028. How China could impact the global biopharma industry. 2022

SCIENTIFIC RESEARCH AND PUBLICATIONS

To develop innovative technologies, China needs groundbreaking research and become one of the brain factories of the world. Significant improvements have been made over the last decades. In 2000 American universities awarded twice as many doctorates in STEM fields (18,289) as Chinese universities (9,038). In 2019 however Chinese universities produced 49,498 PhDs in STEM fields, while American universities produced 33,759, and the gap is increasing.[32] The numbers of scientific research coming out of China are impressive too. The 2022 Nature tables for natural sciences—which includes the physical sciences, chemistry, Earth and environmental sciences and biological sciences—showed

---

[32] Forbes. 2021. U.S. Universities fall further behind China in production of STEM PhDs. https://www.forbes.com/sites/michaeltnietzel/2021/08/07/us-uni versities-fall-behind-china-in-production-of-stem-phds/?sh=15462ca54606. Accessed on October 28, 2023.

that China held the top spot in international publications and surpassed for the first time ever in the United States. In the subcategory of biological sciences, a category formerly referred to as the life sciences in the Nature Index, China ranks second.[33] This shows that Chinese scientists, universities, and research institutes are capable of producing a big volume of scientific research. China also accounted for 27.2% of the most cited papers published in 2018, 2019 and 2020, followed by the United States with 24.9%. This milestone provides evidence that China's scholarship is catching up in quality as well.[34]

That being said, according to Nature magazine's 2021 Nature Index, China hosts only eight of the world's top 100 life sciences institutes, a number which is far behind the United States' 51 and Europe's 28. This indicates that the Chinese researchers contribute big amounts of research, but that at the same time the Chinese contribution to breakthroughs of global significance remains limited. Also, up until 2020 Chinese authors had a lower share of articles than their global peers in leading journals such as Cell, Nature, and Science, and their share of what is called 'core' research—research that constitutes a scientific breakthrough—has remained low.[35] In 2022 in China the total revenue generated from use of IP equaled to US$13 billion. That is only one-tenth of the US where IP generated US$126 billion. This means that China still needs to catch up in developing high-quality patents.

---

[33] Nature. 2023. Nature Index Annual Tables 2023: China tops natural-science table. https://www.nature.com/articles/d41586-023-01868-3. Accessed on October 28, 2023.

[34] Science Insider. 2022. China rises to the first place in most cited papers. https://www.science.org/content/article/china-rises-first-place-most-cited-papers. Accessed on October 28, 2023.

[35] McKinsey & Co. 2022. Vision 2028: How China could impact the global biopharma industry. https://www.mckinsey.com/~/media/mckinsey/industries/life%20sciences/our%20insights/vision%202028%20how%20china%20could%20impact%20the%20global%20biopharma%20industry/vision-2028-how-china-could-impact-the-global-biopharma-industry.pdf. Accessed on October 28, 2023.

Drug Discovery and Artificial Intelligence: Where China Can Leapfrog

By far the most promising way how China could leapfrog in drug discovery and overcome traditional problems, is applying Artificial Intelligence (AI) to the process. Traditional drug discovery research has been well established in the US and Europe. It's however a costly process. In 2021, global pharma invested US$212 billion on R&D, representing an annual growth rate of around 5% since 2013. Yet despite increasing levels of investment, the average length of time it takes novel drugs to reach the market is still over a decade, with an estimated average cost (including drug failures) of US$2.6 billion.[36] These timelines not only delay patient access to innovative therapeutics but also shorten the patent protection period that rewards innovation. Drug discovery is also very risky. Only the top 20% of global pharmaceutical companies worldwide realize a breakeven on their R&D investment after seven years.[37]

With breakthroughs in artificial intelligence, the healthcare industry is undergoing drastic changes. China is no exception and Beijing is very much aware of that. Since 2016, China has issued a series of relevant policies which encouraged and guided the integration of AI, such as natural language processing and machine learning. In 2021, Chinese AI start-ups attracted US$17 billion of private investment, representing one-fifth of the global total.[38] Chinese lawmakers are also encouraging the use of AI in medical applications as they can lead to significant cost reductions and enhanced efficiency. AI-based internet medical and remote medical practices leverage online platforms and software networks to facilitate hospitals and physicians in delivering convenient and efficient healthcare services to patients. On the other hand, Beijing is also starting to impose restrictions on the use of generative AI in online healthcare activities. Personnel who use AI medical devices will likely require professional qualifications.

---

[36] McKinsey & Co. 2019. The pursuit of excellence in new-drug development. https://www.mckinsey.com/industries/life-sciences/our-insights/the-pursuit-of-excellence-in-new-drug-development. Accessed on October 28, 2023.

[37] Medical Expo. 2022. AI poised to take drug discovery to the next level. https://emag.medicalexpo.com/ai-poised-to-take-chinese-drug-discovery-to-the-next-level/. Accessed on October 27, 2023.

[38] Medical Expo. 2022. AI poised to take drug discovery to the next level. https://emag.medicalexpo.com/ai-poised-to-take-chinese-drug-discovery-to-the-next-level/. Accessed on October 27, 2023.

All physicians must undergo real-name authentication to ensure that the medical services are provided by the person themselves. AI medical software is also not permitted to replace doctors in the delivery of medical diagnosis and treatment services.[39]

So unsurprisingly, given the size of the digital economy in China, relevant policies and ramped up investment in healthcare and life science innovation, one area where China starts to become dominant, is in the field of AI-driven drug discovery (AIDD) companies. As China-based breakthrough drug discovery remains relatively slow and as such needs cutting-edge tech to boost it, AI offers a huge opportunity for the Chinese pharmaceutical industry to leapfrog in this field. Integrating AI into China's healthcare and life sciences R&D could add huge economic value in terms of faster drug discovery, optimization of clinical trials and decision-making. As a result, plenty of venture capital has also been flowing into this sector. According to industry reports, financing for AI-assisted drug discovery in China exceeded US$1.26 billion in 2021.[40] 2020 is considered to be 'year one' of AI-driven drug development in China. Before 2020, there were less than ten important domestic players in the field. By the end of 2021, there were more than 60.[41]

Chinese AIDD companies already adopted AI across the drug R&D process. On the 'R' side, AI is being applied in target identification, molecular design and solid-state studies, while on the 'D' side, AI is used in biomarker identification, clinical trial planning and patient recruitment.[42]

---

[39] Lexocology. 2023. Use of artificial intelligence in healthcare industry in mainland China. https://www.lexology.com/library/detail.aspx?g=09f5c7fa-8fc5-4803-9dcd-d96c7ed6d991&utm_source=lexology+daily+newsfeed&utm_medium=html+email+-+body+-+general+section&utm_campaign=lexology+subscriber+daily+feed&utm_content=lexology+daily+newsfeed+2023-09-27&utm_term= . Accessed on September 27, 2023.

[40] ChinaDaily. 2023. AI-powered tech is key to innovation, new drug discovery. https://global.chinadaily.com.cn/a/202204/18/WS625cc8c4a310fd2b29e578aa.html. Accessed on October 28, 2023.

[41] Medical Expo. 2022. AI poised to take drug discovery to the next level. https://emag.medicalexpo.com/ai-poised-to-take-chinese-drug-discovery-to-the-next-level/. Accessed on October 27, 2023.

[42] Medical Expo. 2022. AI poised to take drug discovery to the next level. https://emag.medicalexpo.com/ai-poised-to-take-chinese-drug-discovery-to-the-next-level/. Accessed on October 27, 2023.

At the moment, AI in China is mostly employed in the hit-to-lead stage of drug development, where you screen out the best drug molecule candidates from a large molecule library.

The situation in China's biopharmaceutical industry today is very similar to that of the computer industry in the early 2000s, when the Apple model of 'designed in California, made in China' emerged. Thanks to China's booming CRO infrastructure, AIDD companies which act as discovery and design engines, can design molecules anywhere and then synthesize it and test it in vitro and in vivo in China. These companies no longer have to invest millions in their own labs. Now they can simply outsource which gives them a massive advantage.[43] Companies like Insilico Medicine and XtalPi have in the meantime emerged as important players. Insilico Medicine's evolution and cooperation deals are a good example of how AI has caught on in China. The company was set up in 2014 and has a story from 'death by pilot' to major deals with a highlight of US$80 million upfront in a deal with Exelixis in September 2023.[44] Among others, it has also a six-drug deal worth up to US$1.2 billion with Sanofi to discover candidates for specific targets.[45] Until now no AI drug has hit the market yet, but in June 2023 Insilico Medicine began clinical trials for what they claimed was 'the first fully generative AI drug to reach human clinical trials'.[46]

These points all indicate that AI-driven drug discovery has graduated from exploratory collaborations to serious business and highlights how the company evolved its partnering strategy as biopharmas began acquiring their own AI capabilities. It also shows how China has a unique opportunity to leapfrog in drug discovery, using its unique ecosystem and landscape, and become a global force to be reckoned with. China not

---

[43] Medical Expo. 2022. AI poised to take drug discovery to the next level. https://emag.medicalexpo.com/ai-poised-to-take-chinese-drug-discovery-to-the-next-level/. Accessed on October 27, 2023.

[44] Marketwatch. 2023. Exelixis to license Insilico AI-designed cancer drug. www.marketwatch.com/story/exelixis-to-license-insilico-ai-designed-cancer-drug-5cb62ba7. Accessed on September 27, 2023.

[45] Fierce Biotech. 2022. Amid 'biotech Winter' Insilico turns up the heat with Sanofi deal worth $1.2B in biobucks. www.fiercebiotech.com/biotech/amid-biotech-winter-insilico-turns-heat-sanofi-deal-worth-12b-biobucks. Accessed on September 27, 2023.

[46] Biovox, 2023. AI-discovered drugs will be for sale sooner than you think. https://www.vox.com/future-perfect/23827785/artifical-intelligence-ai-drug-discovery-medicine-pharmaceutical. Accessed on October 27, 2023.

only has a robust digital ecosystem with digital native mindset, but it also has an ample talent supply in computing, chemistry and biology. Especially Europe can fall victim to this trend as the AIDD landscape is being dominated by American and Chinese companies. Europe is still strong in traditional drug discovery, but that advantage might erode quickly if China and the US keep steaming ahead.

Global top 20 AIDD companies by pre-IPO funding

Companies with headquarters in Greater China • Companies with headquarters in ex-Greater China

Company	Hearquarters	Funding $ millons	Company	Hearquarters	Funding $ millons
XtalPi	Greater China	786	Schrodinger	United States	216
Insitro	United States	743	Atomwise	United States	177
Exscientia	United Kingdom	601	Xbiome	Greater China	124
Relay Therapeutics	United States	520	AccutarBio	Greater China	114
Recursion	United States	483	StoneWise	Greater China	110
BenevolentAI	United Kingdom	351	Standigm	Korea	72
Insilico Medicine	Greater China	316	Innoplexus	European Union	64
Owkin	United States	254	Zilliz	Greater China	56
Deep Genomics	Canada	241	Engine Biosciences	United States	53
METiS	Greater China	236	Evaxion Biotech	European Union	41

7
of global top 20 originted from China

31%
funding share by Chinese players

Source McKinsey, Vision 2028. How China could impact the global biopharma industry. 2022

Big Pharma and Chinese Innovation

In a quest to tap into Chinese innovative ecosystem, patients and talents, multinational pharma companies from around the world developed a China R&D strategy. Companies started to set up local R&D hubs, a process that started 20 years ago. There were several reasons to do so. One of the main reasons was the development part within the Research & Development piece. By tapping into the data generated by a nation of 1.3 billion people, it was not only easier to find enough candidates for clinical trials, but the development would also go faster. So, the idea was to bring in drugs under development to China and conduct clinical trials locally to generate quick validation whether a medicine would actually work. At the same time these R&D centers were used to include Chinese sites as a part of global clinical trials. A simultaneous trial globally was not only cheaper to roll out a medicine all over the world, but it was also needed to acquire NMPA approval in order to sell the drugs in China.

In 2004 already, Roche set up a research and early development center which was the first fully owned multinational pharmaceutical R&D center in Shanghai.[47] Sanofi opened its first Asian R&D center in Chengdu in 2018. One of the main focuses of the hub was supporting Sanofi's drug development by managing multi-center clinical trials and accelerating the analysis of trial data.[48] Japan's Shionogi is developing some of its new drugs in China, ahead of Japan, the US and Europe.[49] AstraZeneca (AZ), the largest overseas pharmaceutical company by sales volume in China opened a major global R&D center in Shanghai in 2021. In 2023 AZ had 180 programs under development in China, close to 100% participation in all key global research.[50]

With these global R&D centers, these multinationals foremost pursued a 'China for China' strategy. They primarily use their local R&D centers for support of global clinical trials and supporting development. However, there was also the aspiration of tapping into local innovation and developing drugs in China which then could be rolled out globally. This 'China for global' strategy made perfect sense as Chinese biopharma started to emerge rapidly. So, in fact these big pharma companies wanted to build R&D centers that became the third strategic centers following similar centers in the US and Europe. The results of this strategy, however, are mixed. Roche on its website notes that by the end of 2020, based

---

[47] Roche. 2023. Pharma R&D Shanghai. https://www.roche.com/innovation/structure/rnd-locations/pharma-shanghai. Accessed on November 15, 2023.

[48] Pharmaceutical technology. 2018. Sanofi to open R&D hub in Chengdu, China. https://www.pharmaceutical-technology.com/news/sanofi-research-development-hub-chengdu-china/?cf-view. Accessed on November 15, 2023.

[49] Nikkei Asia. 2023. China's big data draws big pharma. https://asia.nikkei.com/Business/Pharmaceuticals/China-s-big-data-draws-Big-Pharma2. Accessed on November 15, 2023.

[50] China Daily. 2023. AstraZenica returning for sixth consecutive expo. https://www.chinadaily.com.cn/a/202311/06/WS65488e5aa31090682a5eca73.html. Accessed on November 15, 2023.

on the inventions of their China R&D center, 271 patent applications have been filed and 144 had been granted in China, US, EU, or Japan. That is a notable achievement. But it also states at the same time that only nine molecules with contributions from the China site had entered clinical development, which is not a lot.[51] Other MNCs have similar experiences. This in fact means that the multinational pharma companies were not remarkably successful in researching new innovative drugs, using only Chinese R&D sites.

So as local R&D didn't produce the necessary rewards, a different direction had to be taken. International pharma companies embarked on a strategy to partner more with Chinese companies and conclude in-licensing deals. Pharma companies also started to set up their own incubators in China in order to get access to good companies and innovation at a very early stage. The aim is to provide a location for new start-ups without the capital cost of setting up their own lab and office space, with the pharma companies that run them typically providing mentoring and other support that can scale up if their projects gather momentum. It's supposed to be a win-win arrangement. For the pharma companies, it provides an opportunity to get close to new companies and their technologies in the earliest stages, providing an opportunity for partnering later on. For the start-ups it's an advantage to be all under one roof, and at the same are included in the big pharma ecosystem.

AZ established its I·Campus in 2019, a one-stop incubation platform for life science innovation companies.[52] In 2023 Bayer started collaboration with Shanghai Pharmaceuticals for an incubator in Shanghai, focusing on oncology cell and gene therapies.[53] The same year AstraZeneca signed a second collaboration agreement with Hong Kong Science and Technology Parks (HKSTP). The collaboration will involve AstraZeneca and HKSTP supporting and providing services to overseas

---

[51] Roche. 2023. Pharma R&D Shanghai. https://www.roche.com/innovation/structure/rnd-locations/pharma-shanghai. Accessed on November 15, 2023.

[52] China Britain Business Focus. 2020. Astrazeneca China has recently launched a health-tech incubator in Wuxi: the I-Campus. https://focus.cbbc.org/astrazeneca-launch-the-i-campus-health-tech-incubator-in-wuxi/. Accessed on November 30, 2023.

[53] Pharmaphorum. 2023. Bayer adds a new life sciences incubator in China. https://pharmaphorum.com/news/bayer-adds-new-life-science-incubator-china. Accessed on November 15, 2023.

and mainland Chinese start-up companies under the park's incubation program, connecting them to hospitals, KOLs, etc.[54]

This model makes more sense than big pharma setting up their own R&D offices for really frontier research. The old model where multinationals spent years-long, high-cost searches for a blockbuster was already over since long. In Europe and the US it's not big pharma which is driving innovation, bit small pharma companies. In 2020 they accounted for 63% of all new prescription drug approvals over the past five years. Data suggest that emerging biotech companies globally account for more than 70% of the total R&D pipeline.[55] This trend is now also very visible where China's big pharma companies start to cooperate with smaller biopharmas to tap into their innovation, following an 'in China for global' strategy. The idea is that MNCs can partner with Chinese biopharma companies and develop China-originated drugs for the rest of the world.

CHINESE INNOVATION GOES GLOBAL

Despite China not yet developing breakthrough technologies, China-originated biopharma companies are pouring out assets and starting to venture outside China. With innovation going and sometimes local approvals in their hand, Chinese companies started to internationalize and began to run clinical trials abroad to enter the global market. Over the years almost all successful and well-funded Chinese biopharma companies established between 2010 and 2020, have set up offices and R&D centers abroad, mostly in the US. Some have become global players. BeiGene with its operations in the US, China, Europe and Australia for instance was in 2022 conducting more than 90 clinical trials for about

---

[54] SCMP. 2023. Drug giant AstraZeneca teams up with Hong Kong Science Park to drive biotech, medical research growth. https://www.scmp.com/business/china-business/article/3215999/drug-giant-astrazeneca-teams-hong-kong-science-park-drive-biotech-medical-research-growth. Accessed on November 15, 2023.

[55] Pharmavoice. 2020. Small pharma driving big pharma innovation. https://www.pharmavoice.com/news/2020-01-pharma-innovation/612330/ Accessed on November 15, 2023.

30 drugs.[56] It also reached a milestone in 2019 when it received FDA approval for an internally discovered molecule. It was the first China-made cancer drug to earn an FDA breakthrough designation.[57] Overall, in 2018 it was estimated that Chinese companies would submit 20 to 30 new drugs for trials in the US in the next five years.[58]

Unsurprisingly, it were these assets which reached commercialization stage in China since a few years, which came to the attention of global markets. So although Chinese companies mainly still sourced innovations from the global market, striking more than 60 in-licensing partnerships in 2020, an out-licensing trend started to emerge, highlighting the fact that Chinese innovation was going global.[59] Western biopharma companies started to take interest in Chinese developed drugs. Following the new 'in China for global' strategy they increasingly targeted China product/technology innovation to create value ex-China. Tapping into Chinese innovation and in-licensing from China became more and more a common practice. It's a trend that will definitely continue and accelerate in the future. In the innovative drug space, there is a rising number of out-licensing deals from China.

---

[56] China Project. 2022. China's pharma companies are spending big on R&D, but global success remains elusive. https://thechinaproject.com/2022/05/09/chinas-pharma-companies-are-spending-big-on-rd-but-global-success-remains-elusive/. Accessed on November 15, 2022.

[57] FiercePharma. 2019. Beigene nabs landmark FDA nod for Brukinsa, kicking off challenges against blockbuster Imbruvica. https://www.fiercepharma.com/marketing/beigene-nabs-landmark-fda-nod-for-brukinsa-kicking-off-challenge-against-blockbuster. Accessed on November 22, 2023.

[58] The China Project. 2018. 2019: The year Chinese pharma goes big? https://thechinaproject.com/2018/01/03/2019-year-china-pharma-goes-big/. Accessed on November 15, 2023.

[59] McKinsey & Co. 2021. The dawn of China biopharma innovation. https://www.mckinsey.com/industries/life-sciences/our-insights/the-dawn-of-china-biopharma-innovation. Accessed on October 26, 2023.

10 of the biggest deals since 2020

Licensor	Licensee	Asset	Target	Most advanced China stage at closing	Upfront, $ millions	Total deal size, $ millions
BeiGene	Novartis	Tislelizumab	PD-1	Approved	650	2,200
BeiGene	Novartis	Ociperlimab	TIGIT	Phase 2	300	2,895
RemeGen	Seagen	Disitamab vedotin	HER2	Approved	200	2,600
I-MAB	Abbvie	TJC4	CD47	Phase 1b	200	1,940
Innovent	Eli Lilly	Sintilimab	PD-1	Approved	200	1,026
Junshi	Coherus	Toripalimab	PD-1	Approved	150	1,100³
CStone	EQRx	SUgemalimab	PD-L1	Phase 3	146	1,264
Innocare	Biogen	ICP-022⁴	BTK	Phase 2	125	930
Jacobio	Abbvie	JAB-3312	SHP2	Phase 1/2	45	885
Allist	Arrivent	Alflutinib	EGFR	Approved	40	805

Source McKinsey, Vision 2028. How China could impact the global biopharma industry. 2022

As expected most deals revolved around established or next-gen technologies and not breakthrough technologies. In 2020 and 2021 Chinese biotechs signed major out-licensing deals for innovative drugs with MNCs, mainly in oncology, particularly around well-established PD-1 assets.[60] More than half of the deals from 2022 revolve around tumors (including chemoradiotherapy-induced neutropenia) and autoimmune diseases, with deals consisting mainly of monoclonal antibodies, dual antibodies, antibody drug conjugates (ADCs) and CAR-T therapies.[61] One notable exception here is the 2024 deal between Novartis and Argo Biopharmaceutical and Novartis for RNAi therapeutics. It's also

---

[60] McKinsey & Co. 2021. The dawn of China biopharma innovation. https://www.mckinsey.com/industries/life-sciences/our-insights/the-dawn-of-china-biopharma-innovation. Accessed on October 26, 2023.

[61] Echemi. 2023. 2022 License-out inventory: 44 cross-border transactions, with a single maximum amount of nearly US$10 billion; New projects, new technologies... https://www.echemi.com/cms/1147952.html. Accessed on October 26, 2023.

a milestone as it was the first significant overseas out-licensing transaction in the RNAi field from a Chinese biotech company.[62]

Another major push for out-licensing started with the global downturn in the biopharma sector. In China, the growth slowed down in 2022, when the number of IPOs fell significantly. Investors came to expect that the slowdown in new listings of Chinese companies would continue for some time. Without the key influx of cash that equity financing can generate, biopharma companies need to ramp up other activities to generate cash, particularly by out-licensing drugs with the potential for global expansion. In 2021, there were 48 out-licensing deals in China's pharmaceutical industry.[63] In 2022, there were 62 out-licensing deals with foreign companies, with a total value of US$28 billion.[64] One of the highlights in 2023 was the Eccogene-AstraZeneca deal for an oral GLP-1 with a total deal value of US$1.8 billion, including a US$185 million upfront.[65]

---

[62] PR Newswire. 2024. Shanghai Argo announces multi-program RNAi licenses and strategic collaborations with Novartis. https://www.prnewswire.com/news-releases/shanghai-argo-announces-multi-program-rnai-licenses-and-strategic-collaborations-with-novartis-302027699.html. Accessed on January 9, 2024.

[63] Bioworld. 2023. China's biopharma firms need enough cash to get through 'capital winter'. https://www.bioworld.com/articles/697643-chinas-biopharma-firms-need-enough-cash-to-get-through-capital-winter. Accessed on November 26, 2023.

[64] Informaconnect. 2023. China biopharma faces a pause: how bad is it? https://informaconnect.com/china-biopharma-faces-a-pause-how-bad-is-it/. Accessed on November 26, 2023.

[65] Reuters. 2023. AstraZeneca raises stake in obesity drug race with Eccogene deal. www.reuters.com/business/healthcare-pharmaceuticals/astrazeneca-raises-stakes-obesity-drug-race-with-eccogene-deal-2023-11-09/. Accessed on November 28, 2023.

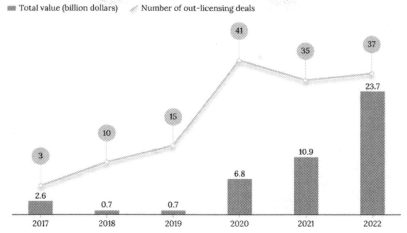

Source Thinkchina. 2023. Cancelled contracts upset Chinese drugmakers' overseas push

ADC Deals from China Skyrocketing

ADCs saw globally a 400% growth in total licensing agreement deal value from 2017 to 2022 and reached a peak of US$16.6 billion in 2022.[66] As China has leapfrogged in the ADC drug development process, there were many eye-catching out-licensing deals involving Chinese companies. In 2023 alone Western biopharma companies have struck at least ten in-licensing or cooperation deals to gain ADC technology from China. These deals accounted for one-third of all the ADC deals being done globally.

ADC leader Seagen—in 2023 acquired by Pfizer for US$43 billion—was the first Western company to in-license an ADC developed in China. In 2021 it acquired ex-Asia rights for an ADC drug from Chinese biotech RemeGen in a deal worth up to $2.6 billion.[67] RemeGen, founded in

---

[66] Pharmaceutical technology. 2023. ADCs dominate with billion dollar licensing agreements in 2022. https://www.pharmaceutical-technology.com/analyst-comment/adcs-huge-licensing-growth-continues/?cf-view. Accessed on November 26, 2023.

[67] Fiercepharma. 2021. In a $2.6B cancer deal, Seagen bets China's first homemade ADC can challenge Roche, AZ-Daiichi. https://www.fiercepharma.com/pharma/taking-aim-at-roche-and-astra-daiichi-seagen-bets-up-to-2-6b-china-s-first-home-made-adc. Accessed on October 20, 2023.

2008 was a pioneer in ADC drug development in China and was the first Chinese biopharma to get an ADC drug into human studies.[68] Most spectacular were the three ADC agreements in 2022 between Merck and Kelun-Biotech which stipulated that the two companies will develop seven ADCs for cancer in a deal worth up to US$9.3 billion, including a US$175 million upfront.[69] Despite Merck in 2023 abandoning the joint development of two candidate ADC drugs which had yet to start clinical trials, the deal still remains very significant.[70] BioNTech is banking heavily on China. It closed a deal with Duality Biologics which out-licensed global rights (ex-China) for two self-developed ADC candidates, in a deal worth up to US$1.5 billion and another one with MediLink Therapeutics.[71] Lanova Medicines entered into an exclusive license agreement with an upfront of US$25 Million with US-based Turning Point Therapeutics.[72] In 2023 Hansoh Pharma sold ex-China rights to GSK in a US$1.57 billion deal[73] and US-based Aiolos Bio announced a US$245 million series A, to develop further a phase II trial for its lead asset to

---

[68] PharmaExec. 2018. Antibody–drug conjugates in China. https://www.pharmexec.com/view/antibody-drug-conjugates-china. Accessed on October 26, 2023.

[69] Fiercebiotech. 2023. Merck puts eye-popping $9.3B on the line in lopsided ADC deal with Kelun-Biotech. https://www.fiercebiotech.com/biotech/merck-writes-eye-popping-93b-blank-check-biobucks-deal-3rd-kelun-biotech-adc-deal. Accessed on October 26, 2023.

[70] Reuters. 2023. Merck discontinues some cancer drug development with China's Sichuan Kelun. https://www.reuters.com/business/healthcare-pharmaceuticals/merck-discontinues-some-cancer-drug-development-with-chinas-sichuan-kelun-2023-10-23/. Accessed on October 26, 2023.

[71] Medicitynews. 2023. BioNTech turns to China again for cancer drugs, paying $70 million to partner on an ADC. https://medcitynews.com/2023/10/biontech-turns-to-china-again-for-cancer-drugs-paying-70m-to-partner-on-an-adc/. Accessed on November 26, 2023.

[72] MDQ Ventures. 2023. Global ADC drug development & China opportunities. https://msqventures.com/global-adc-drug-development-china-opportunities-report. Accessed on October 26, 2023.

[73] Fiercebiotech. 2023. In a 2nd big ADC deal of the day, GSK inks $1.4B pact for Hansoh gynecology cancer asset. https://www.fiercebiotech.com/biotech/2nd-big-adc-deal-day-gsk-inks-2b-pact-hansoh-gynecology-cancer-asset. Accessed on October 26, 2023.

treat severe asthma, an anti-TSLP antibody licensed from Jiangsu Hengrui Pharmaceuticals.[74]

All these deals show that there is not only quality to be found in China, but that arguably this field is becoming very crowded now also. This starts to effect innovation in the US and Europe also. When attending BioEurope in November 2023, several European life sciences investors claimed not to be investing anymore in European ADC companies as China had surpassed them. Instead, they were now contemplating investing in Chinese ADC companies. This also means that any foreign ADC company needs to raise the bar in order to compete.

CAR-T Therapies Are Next

CAR-T cells could be—and possibly should be—the next opportunity for China's homegrown innovation to go global. The world has witnessed a boom of gene and cell therapy (GCT) over the last years, and GCT has been proven a new modality for treating incurable diseases like cancer. With more than 400 cell therapies in clinical trials in China, the country ranks second only after the US.[75] As mentioned, especially in CAR-T therapy—one of the subsegments in CGT therapy—China is making headways. Chimeric antigen receptor (CAR) T-cell therapy is a novel and effective therapeutic approach that has emerged to revolutionize cancer treatment, especially for blood cancers. The US pioneered the development of CAR-T industry, resulting in the first CAR-T therapy being approved by the FDA in 2017.[76] But from the mid-2010s China started to catch up with the US. From 2018 to 2021, Chinese cell therapy companies have raised approximately US$2.4 billion in funding, growing at a compound annual growth rate of 45%. By 2022 two CAR-T products had been approved by the NMPA, from joint venture Fosun

---

[74] Businesswire. 2023. Aiolos Bio launches with $245 Million Series A investment to advance development of novel. Phase-2 ready TSLP antibody. https://www.businesswire.com/news/home/20231024577944/en/Aiolos-Bio-Launches-with-245-Million-Series-A-Investment-to-Advance-Development-of-Novel-Phase-2-Ready-TSLP-Antibody. Accessed on October 26, 2023.

[75] Yahoo Finance. 2023. China cell therapy market size clinical trials companies insight. https://finance.yahoo.com/news/china-cell-therapy-market-size-114500734.html. Accessed on October 26, 2023.

[76] Equal Ocean. 2023. Car-T therapy market map in China. https://equalocean.com/analysis/2023011619378. Accessed on October 26, 2023.

Kite and JW Therapeutics.[77] China-originated players have also made breakthroughs and caught up with global players. One of the very first eye opening deals was concluded in 2017 when Janssen Biotech (part of Johnson & Johnson) entered into a worldwide collaboration and license agreement with Legend Biotech to develop, manufacture and commercialize a CAR T-cell drug candidate.[78] Legend Biotech, IASO Biotherapeutics and CARsgen Therapeutics all received NDA acceptance of their BCMA CAR-T products, making them the global top companies in BCMA CAR-T therapy. CARsgen Therapeutics is a global leader in solid tumors and its CT041 is the world's first CAR-T candidate for the treatment of solid tumors entering Phase II clinical trial.[79]

The development of CAR-T therapies in China now outpaces research happening in the West. Moreover, for each CAR-T therapy developed by US companies, there are 1.5 times more CAR-T therapies being investigated by Chinese companies. This means that of the ten companies involved in the development of CAR-T drugs, six are based in China.[80] This all means that in the field of cell therapy China is poised to successfully conclude more international partnerships and out-licensing deals.

Percentage of clinical trials for CAR-T Therapies per country.

---

[77] Equal Ocean. 2023. Car-T therapy market map in China. https://equalocean.com/analysis/2023011619378. Accessed on October 26, 2023.

[78] Johnson & Johnson. 2017. Janssen Enters Worldwide Collaboration and License Agreement with Chinese Company Legend Biotech to Develop Investigational CAR-T Anti-Cancer Therapy. https://www.jnj.com/media-center/press-releases/janssen-enters-worldwide-collaboration-and-license-agreement-with-chinese-company-legend-biotech-to-develop-investigational-car-t-anti-cancer-therapy. Accessed on October 26, 2023.

[79] CARSGen Therapeutics. 2023. CARsgen Initiates Phase 2 Clinical Trial for CLDN18.2 CAR T-cell Product CT041 in the U.S. https://www.carsgen.com/en/news/2023-05-18/ Accessed on October 26, 2023.

[80] Clinical Trials Arena. 2023. China dominates CAR-T Therapies. www.clinicaltrialsarena.com/comment/china-car-t-therapies/?cf-view&cf-closed. Accessed on November 22, 2023.

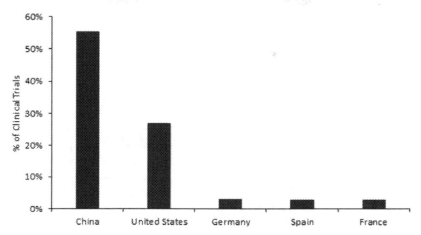

Source Clinical Trials Arena. 2023. China dominates CAR-T Therapies

What Will the Future Bring?

China is already clearly an important and integral part of the global biopharma industry, and not a separate ecosystem anymore. China has a big market, good scientists, a big pool of talent, and the capital to foster innovation. Chinese companies now invest increasingly in R&D. It's a well-established fact that China developed assets start to make breakthroughs internationally. Chinese homegrown innovation definitely starts to come of age. In 2022 the global commercial value of the top ten China-originated products reached US$2 billion in sales abroad and at home. Over the last years, China-originated innovation is increasingly seeking global value. Since 2021 Chinese biopharmas annually close around 30 out-licensing deals. They are also globally expanding through an increasing amount of FDA/EMEA registrations. Despite the biotech Winter, there is still a continued momentum of China-originated innovation with vast amounts of INDs and NDAs. This proves the robustness of the sector. Chinese companies also increasingly invest in R&D. In 2021, among A-share and Hong Kong-listed pharma companies, 247 invested more than US$15 million in R&D and 25 invested more than US$150 million. BeiGene was the forerunner and spent US$1.43 billion, followed by Hengrui which spent US$930 million.[81]

The innovation potential of China is now unquestioned. Given the fact that the Chinese biopharma sector only exists for not yet a decade, this is a remarkable achievement. But despite having great strides going forward, Chinese biopharma has yet to produce a substantial number of patented drugs that can compete globally and be commercialized around the world. This is of course not unusual as it takes years to develop new drugs, while the Chinese biopharma sector is still relatively young. Despite China-originated medicines being commercialized abroad, most of them captured a limited amount of global value. That also means investors are not interested anymore in me-too products, as their commercial value is limited. They will now only invest if assets are globally in the top three by development status or have a clear differentiation potential.

The real question is how quickly China developed assets will achieve best-in-class and even first-in-class status. As many local innovators pivot toward globally competitive innovation, several capabilities need to be upgraded. China still has gaps in academic and scientific research, drug discovery and the infrastructure for translating academic research to drugs. A more robust global clinical development, more thoughtful clinical trial design and regulatory strategy are also needed. The question is thus whether China biopharma companies will be able to develop quickly a reputation for disruptive breakthrough therapies. Despite holding overall positive views about future innovation in China, it is yet to be seen whether Chinese companies can match any of the high-profile breakthrough innovations in Europe or the US. A McKinsey survey from 2022 revealed that two-thirds of Chinese executives think they and other China-originated companies will have best-in-class or first-in-class biopharma assets in Western markets by 2028, while fewer than a third of non-Chinese executives expect this to happen.[82] China might not yet

---

[81] China Project 2022. China's pharma companies are spending big on R&D, but global success remains elusive. https://thechinaproject.com/2022/05/09/chinas-pharma-companies-are-spending-big-on-rd-but-global-success-remains-elusive/. Accessed on November 15, 2022.

[82] McKinsey & Co. 2022. Vision 2028: How China could impact the global biopharma industry. https://www.mckinsey.com/~/media/mckinsey/industries/life%20sciences/our%20insights/vision%202028%20how%20china%20could%20impact%20the%20global%20biopharma%20industry/vision-2028-how-china-could-impact-the-global-biopharma-industry.pdf. Accessed on October 28, 2023.

be top-notch in frontier innovation and groundbreaking research, but they are very capable to improve and optimize existing research and technologies. In other words, if a scientific problem can be changed into an engineering problem, Chinese biopharmas can develop assets with world-class potential. Within the R&D space, currently Chinese companies are particularly good at the 'D' part, but still need to improve on the 'R' part. China's current strength is innovation on innovation, but that might evolve rapidly into real frontier innovation. China can significantly disrupt the value chain, for example through AI and the leverage of the scale of the China ecosystem, and affordable innovation.

The Art of the Biopharma Deal: The China Angle

Abstract Over the last years foreign companies have been very active in partnership and cooperation deals with Chinese biopharma companies and healthcare investors. Anybody who wants to raise money from Chinese investors or strike a partnering or cooperation deal with Chinese companies however, needs to understand what investors or Chinese pharma companies are looking for. And because of the vast differences and needs of the Chinese healthcare and pharmaceutical market, the value proposition towards China can be very different than other markets. The most reputable and well-known USD-denominated healthcare funds in China are originally from the US, but have very specific funds to invest in China or ex-US. Then there are the strategic investors who are actively investing in, and in-licensing assets from foreign companies. There are mainly two categories of strategic investors: the newly established, venture capital backed biopharma companies, and the traditional Chinese pharmaceutical companies. It's important to understand the background of these companies. The traditional pharma companies are not rooted in innovation, and as such are not always that familiar with the process of drug discovery. The newly established biopharma companies on the other hand are well versed in innovation, but of course don't have the established sales network as the big pharma companies. Just like the US or Europe, Chinese investors have also engaged in incubating or building new biopharma companies. As a matter of fact at the height of the biotech investment boom, almost all Chinese biotechs have been incubated by

© The Author(s), under exclusive license to Springer Nature Singapore Pte Ltd. 2024
S. Agten and B. Wu, *Biopharma in China*,
https://doi.org/10.1007/978-981-97-1471-1_5

healthcare venture capitalists, and were not spun out from universities or research institutes, as is often the case in the US or Europe.. As such it's important to understand that incubation or new venture building in China is fundamentally different than in Europe or the US. Lastly it's important to understand what diseases are more prevalent in China, or which technologies are more needed than others.

Keywords China angle · Foreign Direct Investment (FDI) · Fund · Incubation · In-licensing · Investment · Partnering · Regional rights · Strategic investor · Value proposition

Anybody who wants to raise money from Chinese investors or strike a partnering or cooperation deal with Chinese companies, needs to understand what investors or Chinese pharma companies are looking for. And because of the vast differences and needs of the Chinese healthcare and pharmaceutical market, the value proposition towards China can be very different than other markets.

Chinese Financial Investors

Just like the US and Europe, also in China, there are different kinds of venture capitalist firms. It's important to make a distinction between US and RMB denominated funds. As China still adheres to a strict capital control policy, this means that USD funds can freely invest all over the world without limitations, while RMB-denominated funds need to go through a Foreign Direct Investment (FDI) procedure to get official approval to invest outside China.

The most reputable and well-known USD-denominated healthcare funds in China are originally from the US, but have very specific funds to invest in China or ex-US. Orbimed Asia, Eight Roads (Fidelity), Lilly Asia Ventures, Sequoia Capital China or Vivo Capital are a few of the best examples. These funds often work in close cooperation together with their US counterparts, and tap into a global network of companies and KOLs. Equally sophisticated and also with a global reach, are reputable Chinese life sciences funds like CBC Group, Quan Capital (connected to Zai Lab), Nanfung Life Sciences, Qiming Venture Partners, Lyfe Capital or Hillhouse Capital. They often manage several multi-billion dollar funds, and have a wide portfolio of healthcare and other tech companies. All of these funds are backed by institutional investors, big MNCs in the pharmaceutical industry or other sectors, family offices, or well-known Chinese companies. Their LPs could range from IKEA, US or European pension funds, and so forth.[1] Qiming Venture Partners, for instance, founded in 2006, manages seven RMB funds and 11 US dollar funds. They have offices in Shanghai, Beijing, Suzhou, Hong Kong, Seattle, Boston, and the San Francisco Bay Area.[2] Altogether it has US$9.4 billion under management. In its portfolio of 500+ companies, it has 180 healthcare firms, and the bulk of its overall investments are in so-called Series A or B rounds.[3]

Despite these funds mostly being China originated, they are active globally, but mainly in the US, where they have offices and a strong network. All these top funds are also extremely knowledgeable. Most of these funds have offices in China and the US and are in fact acting more like US investors with a global vision. They are very much focused on the latest technologies and invest in companies with global potential. Moreover, despite the global downturn and tougher conditions, these large investment companies are able to continue to raise large sums of funds, showing their capabilities. Qiming Ventures for instance closed in 2022 two new China technology and healthcare funds with US$3.2 billion in fresh capital. In 2022 in total US$12 billion in new funds from Orbimed Asia, Sequioa Capital, Qiming and Vivo Capital for future investments were announced.[4]

Important to understand is that most China-originated funds typically don't lead investment rounds abroad, but are happy to act as follow-on investors, especially when a reputable US or European healthcare fund

---

[1] Private Equity International. 2022. Healthcare fund CBC eyes global expansion after closing flagship above hard-cap. www.privateequityinternational.com/healthcare-firm-cbc-eyes-global-expansion-after-closing-flagship-above-hard-cap/. Accessed on November 29, 2023.

[2] Qiming Venture Partners. 2023. About. https://www.qimingvc.com/en/about. Accessed on November 29, 2023.

[3] Reuters. 2022. 'Overinvested' China healthcare sector set up for shake up, top venture fund says. https://www.reuters.com/world/china/overinvested-china-healthcare-sector-set-shake-up-top-venture-fund-2022-09-27/. Accessed on November 29, 2023.

[4] ChinaBio. 2022. 2022 Life sciences deals: Slow start, late recovery: Top 10 deals worth $21.5 billion. http://www.chinabiotoday.com/articles/2022-life-science-deals. Accessed on December 23, 2023.

is the lead investor. Almost all the investors are most likely to invest in later-stage investment rounds. When investing abroad, they rarely would invest in a Seed-series or A-Series. Most of these funds are big, that their minimum investment ticket is at least US$ five to ten million, often even starting from US$20 million. Furthermore, as their home turf is still mostly China, they need more convincing to invest abroad. This is especially true for investing in Europe. Almost all China originated, but global investors are familiar with the US, its companies, and investors. Universities like Harvard or MIT are also well known. This is less true for European top research institutes or top biopharma companies, which are definitely less known in China.

**Most Active China Investors into
US and European Venture-Backed Companies
Number of Deals (2018–2020)**

Venture Capital		Corporate Investor	
17	QIMING VENTURE PARTNERS	15	WuXi AppTec
14	DECHENG CAPITAL	9	Lilly Asia Ventures
11	SEQUOIA CAPITAL CHINA	8	Baidu
10	6 Dimensions Capital	6	YONGHUA CAPITAL
7	VI Ventures	5	Tencent
6*	COWIN VENTURE	4	PING AN HEALTH
6*	EFUNG CAPITAL		

Source Silicon Valley Bank, 2020. China in the global healthcare system

Chinese Strategic Investors

Besides the healthcare venture capitalists, there are also strategic investors who are actively investing in, and in-licensing assets from foreign companies. There are mainly two categories of strategic investors: the newly established, venture capital backed biopharma companies, and the traditional Chinese pharmaceutical companies. Uniquely to China, by far most of the biopharma companies were established to in-license assets from abroad. As such they were more acting as strategic, than as biotechs with core R&D capabilities. Dealing with a well-funded but newly established Chinese biopharma has advantages and disadvantages. As founders of the company are typically internationally experienced pharma executives with good English languages, they understand well how to successfully conclude an in-licensing deal, and how to deal with foreign companies in general. Furthermore they have experience in conducting clinical trials, and understand how innovation works. They also have relatively experienced healthcare investors, and a drive to create value rapidly. One of the main drawbacks, however, is that these biotechs don't have established sales channels, and little to no experience in dealing with the NMPA. They are not fully vertically integrated, which limits their strategic capabilities.

The Chinese pharmaceutical companies, on the other hand, are on paper a more suitable party to partner with in China. It is however important to understand the background of these companies. As the government is pursuing a policy of upgrading production facilities, providing better quality drugs, and at the same keeping prices under control, local pharma companies are increasingly facing financial and regulatory pressure. In order to remain competitive, not only do they need to up their game, but at the same time they need to turn away from generic medicines and move increasingly toward the development of innovative medicines. The latter is not so easy for them. By far most of the traditional pharma companies are not familiar at all with innovation and R&D, and as such have difficulties to really understand how the process of innovation works. We estimate that there are only 50 Chinese pharmaceutical companies which are able to properly assess and in-license innovative medicines. Companies like Hengrui, Fosun Pharma, Grand Pharma or Hansoh Pharma, started the innovation journey already years ago. They are well versed in innovation and the potential it can bring. Amomg the more traditional companies, they are however the exception, not the rule.

In contrast, most pharmaceutical companies not very familiar with innovation, originated as family-owned business, and were set up in a period where quality or innovation were almost alien concepts. Innovation is simply not in their DNA. Furthermore many of these companies are still very much top-down managed, and decisions are often taken by the owner alone. Most owners however are good businessmen, but often didn't enjoy a proper education, let alone are they versed in biology or chemistry. That means that for them it's really difficult to understand the real value of an innovative drug, and as such find it also difficult to pay market prices in order to in-license medicines. Moreover as they are not very familiar with the international markets, and often lack English language skills, it's sometimes very difficult to come to an agreement with them. Despite these problems, the main advantages to work with these pharma companies is that many of them are vertically integrated. Most of them have their own production facilities, and their own sales force. Their sales network often covers thousands of hospitals. This means that many of these companies will have problems in dealing with innovative drugs, but once marketed, they are good partners to drive sales.

Venture Building and Incubation

Just like the US or Europe, Chinese investors have engaged in incubating or building new biopharma companies. As a matter of fact at the height of the biotech investment boom, almost all Chinese biotechs have been incubated by healthcare venture capitalists. As such it's important to understand that incubation or new venture building in China is fundamentally different than in Europe or the US. In China, investors worked together with biotech entrepreneurs to establish a new company. And one of their first tasks was to in-license technology or drugs to fill the pipeline and create value. In the US or Europe on the other hand, very often new biotechs are being created as spin-offs from universities or research institutions. This also explains partly why investors in China take a much more hands-on approach in managing the development of the ventures. As they didn't rely on the skills of the entrepreneur, but more on the technology in-licensed or acquired from abroad, they had a bigger leverage.

Source Agio Capital, Biopharma in China, a pivot to Europe. 2023

Some Chinese companies preferred a more direct approach to expand the pipeline of their company. The Chinese company Harbour Biomed is such an example. The company was set up in 2016 with a base in Shanghai and US$50 million from two China-focused venture investment firms, Advantech Capital and Legend Capital. The first thing they did was to buy Erasmus University spin-out Harbour Antibodies in Rotterdam, which gave them two transgenic mouse platforms for the discovery of fully human antibodies.[5] As Harbour Biomed had capital available, but no own proprietary technology, the easiest way for them was to acquire a technology platform abroad. The same goes for the 2021 acquisition where China-based Worg Pharmaceuticals acquired the technology platform and all the assets of the Belgian biotech Apitope with a focus on autoimmune diseases.[6] The acquisition enabled Worg to integrate the technology into its own company and develop global IP based on European technology.

As Chinese financial and strategic investors were looking to build new companies in China, they were also very much open to build joint ventures in China. In this context incubation has in reality a lot of meanings. Mostly it means that the Chinese investors wanted to build a new company in China, using foreign technology. Typically a foreign company brings in its assets or technology platform into the newco, which is then funded by China-originated investors, run by a mostly Chinese team. The idea is that cutting-edge technology can be brought rapidly to the

---

[5] Dealmaker. 2023. Harbour Biomed. www.dealmaker.nl/company/harbour-biomed. Accessed on December 23, 2023.

[6] Bioville 2021. Worg Pharma to acquire Apitope. https://bioville.be/en/news/worg-pharma-to-acquire-apitope/,. Accessed on January 5, 2024.

Chinese market in a novel way. The Chinese investors use their strengths, which are deploying capital and bringing an experienced team on board. The foreign party uses its strength, which is its technology and applying its R&D capabilities.

This model has several advantages. First of all the foreign company gets access to the Chinese market, without the need to set up a local presence. Moreover the foreign mother company gets rewarded in upfront and/or license payments and typically also a significant equity stake in the newco. Especially receiving equity is interesting as the upside is potentially much greater than a straightforward licensing deal. If the newco licenses or acquires the rights of the platform technology from the mother company, it then can be used to develop new assets in China. This means that the newco can develop drugs with a regional or global potential, depending on the agreement with the technology provider. The newco can even grow faster than the mother company. It can generate quicker clinical validation for drugs under development as the Chinese ecosystem lends itself to faster clinical results. This in turn ensures that the company can follow a development path which leads to an IPO in Hong Kong, Shenzhen or Shanghai, or acquisition by another company. And all this completely independent from the mother company. With this kind of model the foreign biopharma really taps into China as a source of capital, rapid clinical development, and further development of its pipeline.

This concept has been implemented successfully over the years, mostly between US biotech companies and Chinese investors. One of the first examples was successfully set up in 2018 when Danish Ascendis Pharma set up a newco in China with VIVO Capital. Both parties received an equal equity share in the newly incubated company, while VIVO Capital contributed almost all of the funding. Other newcos were set up by giants like Hillhouse Capital, Orbimed Asia or Nanfung Life Sciences. Although this incubation model still exists, it has become less used, mainly because most investors have shifted investments toward companies which have global potential, which most of these newcos don't have. Usually, the assets contributed to the newco carried regional rights, not necessarily global rights. One of the last examples was Arrowhead Pharmaceuticals (NASDAQ: ARWR) which in 2022 set up a newco in China. The newco raised US$60 million for the development of Arrowhead's four early-stage cardio-metabolic RNAi assets. Belgian mRNA company eTheRNA set up their joint venture with Chinese pharma company Grand Pharma in China, while Grand Pharma also contributed to the B-Series of eTheRNA.

NewCo	Found Yr.	Founding Biotech	Lead Investor (founding)	Capital	Ownership at Founding	Therapeutic Area	Assets at Founding
Visen Pharma	2018	Ascendis Pharma HQ in Denmark Nasdaq: ASND	Vivo Capital	$40M Series A $150M Series	Ascendis 50% Vivo 50%	Endocrine	3x Assets License for Greater China
BIOSHIN	2020	Biohaven NYSE (BHVN)	Orbimed	$60M Series A	Undisclosed	CNS	Asia Pac rights rimegepant (Ph3)
ZENTERA	2020	Zentalis NASDAQ (ZNTL)	Tybourne Capital	$20M Series A $75M Series B	Zentalis 60% investors 40%	Oncology (Small Molecules)	3x Assets in Ph 1 & 2
Overland ADCT	2020	ADC Therapeutics Swiss Biotech NASDAQ: ADCT	Hillhouse Capital	$50M	Hillhouse 51% ADC Therapeutics 49%	Oncology (ADC)	4X Assets (PH: 3/2, Preclinical) For China and Singapore
Allogene Overland Biopharma	2020	Allogene Therapeutics NASDAQ GS: ALLO	Hillhouse Capital	$117M($40M goes to Allogene)	Hillhouse 51% Allogene 49%	Oncology (Allogenic CAR-T)	Allo-CAR T, Ph 1 China, TW, S Kr and SG $40M upfront
Lian Bio	2020	MyoKardia, Navire Pharma and OED Therapeutics	Perceptive Advisors	2020 Series A, $310M IPO 2021 NASDAQ: $325M	Undisclosed	Cardiology & Oncology	PRC, HK and Macau 3 Assets 2x Ph3, 1x Ph1
Ignis Therapeutics	2021	SK Biopharm Korea SKBP(326030)	6 Dimensions Capital	$180M Series A	SK Bio >50% 6 Dim <50%	CNS	5 assets (2 FDA approved) $20M upfront, 6(3 M milestone & royalties)
NeuroFront	2021	Neurokell Israel-based	Nan Fung Life Sciences & Pivotal Bioventure	Not Disclosed	Not Disclosed	CNS Devices	One medical devices, Greater China and S Korea
Zenas Biopharma	2021	Dianthus Therapeutics & Xencor (NASDAQ: XNCR)	Tellus BioVentures & Fairmount Funds	Undisclosed	Undisclosed	Immunology	Zenas owns worldwide rights to 3 of the 7 assets
SanReno Therapeutics	2021	Chinook Therapeutics (NASDAQ:KDNY)	Frazier Healthcare US, Pivotal bioVenture China	$40M	Chinook 50% Investors 50%	Rare Kidney Diseases	Two Assets: Ph3 & Ph1 PRC, HK, Macau, TW & SG
Visirna Therapeutics	2022	Arrowhead Pharmaceuticals (NASDAQ:ARWR)	Vivo Capital	$60M Seed Round	Vivo <50% Arrowhead >50%	Cardio-metabolics RNAi	4x Early-Stage Assets For Greater China

Source Agio Capital, Biopharma in China, a pivot to Europe. 2023

The China Angle

As mentioned, despite Chinese financial investors looking for a return in investment, they very often also have a strategic view. They like to invest in companies which have a specific edge in the Chinese market. Most Chinese healthcare VCs have a portfolio of companies and have a strong tendency to build synergies between these portfolio companies. This means that VC and PE funds can invest themselves, but at the same will introduce their portfolio companies which then in turn could potentially cooperate with the foreign company. So in this aspect working with China-based VC funds also brings partnering opportunities. In this way Chinese healthcare funds act differently compared to a typical European fund or US-based fund. This also means that any foreign company needs to develop a specific 'China angle', and needs to have a very specific positioning toward Chinese investors. And as the Chinese biopharma sector is developing rapidly, the value proposition changes also accordingly. Finding the right value proposition for China is not always easy. Most Western biopharma companies have a good understanding of what their unique value proposition is for the well-known US and European markets. When it comes to China however, most foreign biotechs have a much lesser understanding of the specific requirements and problems that Chinese patients or hospitals face, what diseases are more prevalent than others, or what solutions are needed. This is also the reason why every company should analyze carefully whether the Chinese market is a good fit, before starting any endeavor toward China. Generally speaking, it's important to bring really innovative products and technologies to the Chinese market. The so called 'me-too' or 'me-better' products or technologies are not of interest to Chinese companies or investors anymore.

When talking about product market fit, it's important to look at the disease burden in China. There are significant differences in the prevalence of diseases in China compared to other parts of the world. Just like in the Western world, cancer is a big problem In China. There are however differences in prevalence. Due to bigger amount of air pollution in China the most common cancer is lung cancer, while in the US breast cancer is the number one cancer.[7] There are also genetic differences. Melanoma is about 20 times more common in white people than in black people. Also in China melanoma is a rare malignant tumor.[8] Several screening technologies and strategies have been developed to reduce the cancer burden in the US. In China, however, considering the large population, potential benefits and harms from screening and the less developed capacity of health services, the process of systematic cancer screening is still much less developed. As such there is a more urgent need for cancer screening technologies in China than in the US or Europe.

Rapid economic growth in China has been accompanied by an alarming rise of certain diseases. The Chinese growing middle class has a much more Western lifestyle, which in turn leads to all kinds of problems. Diabetes is a growing problem. There are however significant differences which are important to understand when approaching the Chinese market. Type 1 diabetes for instance is much less common in China than

---

[7] National Library of Medicine. 2022. Cancer statistics in China and the United States, 2022: profiles, trends and determinants. https://www.ncbi.nlm.nih.gov/pmc/articles/PMC8920425/#:~:text=In%202022%2C%20there%20will%20be,of%20cancer%20death%20in%20both. Accessed on December 22, 2023.

[8] National Library of Medicine. 2022. Cancer statistics in China and the United States, 2022: Profiles, trends and determinants. https://www.ncbi.nlm.nih.gov/pmc/articles/PMC8920425/#:~:text=In%202022%2C%20there%20will%20be,of%20cancer%20death%20in%20both. Accessed on December 22, 2023.

in the Western world. While compared with European descents, Chinese patients with Type 2 diabetes are diagnosed at a relatively young age and low BMI.[9] Also in the autoimmune spaces there are significant differences. Worldwide a total of 2.8 million people are estimated to live with multiple sclerosis (MS) (35.9 per 100,000 population).[10] Despite MS being a well-known disease in Europe and the US, typically in Asia, the disease is much less common. In China the disease is also very much underdiagnosed.[11] As such new innovative treatments of MS might have a strong potential in the US and Europe, in China the appeal will be less.

As innovation in the Chinese biopharma sector is relatively new, cutting edge technologies are often still in early stage of development. Therefore Chinese financial and strategic investors are not only looking to in-license assets, they are increasingly looking for technology cooperations. Among these, cutting-edge technologies in the fields of protein degradation, radiopharmaceuticals, and everything RNA related have a good potential in China. Just like in the rest of the world Chinese biopharma companies are for instance looking for new LNP delivery technologies. Spurred on by the Covid-19 pandemic, new technologies to combat infectious diseases are of strategic important in China, and thus very much welcomed. With a population of over 1.3 billion and 50% of the world's livestock,[12] China's ecology poses a risk for emerging, re-emerging, and novel infectious diseases that could threaten China and the

---

[9] National Library of Medicine. 2019. Meeting the challenge of diabetes in China. https://www.ncbi.nlm.nih.gov/pmc/articles/PMC7054646/. Accessed on December 2, 2023.

[10] National Library of Medicine. 2020. Rising prevalence of multiple sclerosis worldwide: Insights from the Atlas of MS, third edition. www.ncbi.nlm.nih.gov/pmc/articles/PMC7720355/#:~:text=A%20total%20of%202.8%20million,gaps%20in%20prevalence%20estimates%20persist. Accessed on December 5, 2023.

[11] National Library of Medicine. 2022. The incidence, of prevalence, diagnosis and treatment of multiple sclerosis in China: A narrative review. www.ncbi.nlm.nih.gov/pmc/articles/PMC9349092/#:~:text=The%20first%20nationwide%20study%20reported,Quality%20Monitoring%20System%20%5B10%5D. Accessed on December 2, 2023.

[12] ScienceAdvances. 2018. China's livestock transition: Driving forces, impacts and consequences. https://www.science.org/doi/10.1126/sciadv.aar8534. Accessed on December 4, 2023.

rest of the world. In 2021 more than six million cases of notifiable infectious diseases were reported in China. HFMD, Hepatitis B and infectious diarrhea were among the most viral ones. The three diseases accounted for 53.95% of all the diseases.

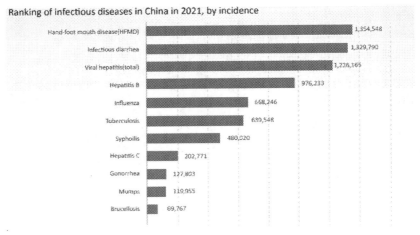

Ranking of infectious diseases in China in 2021, by incidence

Source Statista, 2022. Infectious diseases China, 2021.

End of the First Cycle, 2022 and Beyond: A Drastic Reset, Increased Challenges But Also New Opportunities

Abstract In the biopharma sector, China has experienced its first boom and bust cycle. Prior to 2017 there was an emergence phase with a wave of innovation. Between the period 2018–2022 we witnessed a growth phase, catalyzed by even more funding and new IPO channels in Hong Kong and Shanghai. 2022 saw the start of a reset phase characterized by a drastic market correction, in line with global biotech trends. Companies and healthcare funds alike need to reposition themselves for the future, as funding is more difficult and budgets get tighter. The downturn also challenges the fundamentals of value creation and reveals major ecosystem gaps in China. At the same time government policies promote 'Common Prosperity', which is pushing prices for innovative drugs down, which in turn decreases profits, and hurts investors' sentiments. Affordable innovation is now key. Geopolitics also play an increasing role, hurting prospects of Chinese companies to become global players. That being said, the long-term perspectives look good. The Chinese innovation ecosystem is showing signs of resilience, and Chinese biopharma companies are moving increasingly to real first-in-class drug development, hence slowly but steadily becoming globally competitive. A clear 'going global' trend is prevalent. The Chinese innovative pharma market is also still a growth story and has ample room for expansion. Despite this however, the internationalization of Chinese homegrown innovative drugs will still have many hurdles to take. But China is increasingly playing an important role in global drug competition and innovation. As such Western biopharma companies will face new challenges in their home markets. If Chinese biopharma companies succeed in developing the same quality medicine, but at a much more affordable price, they can sell their drugs in foreign markets and compete head-on with the competition abroad. This however doesn't mean that Chinese drugmakers are in a position to set up large organizations abroad, like the Western MNCs. The most promising way now for them to launch China-originated drugs abroad, is via international partnerships. This means that foreign companies should embrace a strategy of 'innovating with China', or 'in China for global'.

Keywords Affordable innovation · Anti-corruption · Boom and bust cycle · Common prosperity · Global potential · Geopolitics · Going global · Health economics · Protectionism · Reimbursement

After the explosive growth starting around a decade ago, currently the Chinese biopharma sector is experiencing its first full cycle of boom and bust. During the 2023 China Healthcare Summit, McKinsey identified three significant phases, all with its own distinct characteristics. Prior to 2017 there was an emergence phase with a wave of innovation accelerated by regulatory integration, sufficient funding by specialized funds and inflow of Chinese talents from overseas, the so-called 'returnees'. Between the period 2018 to 2022 we witnessed the exuberance phase, catalyzed by even more funding—now by more generalist investors—, and new IPO channels in Hong Kong and Shanghai. 2022 saw the start of a reset phase characterized by a drastic market correction, in line with global biotech trends.

Difference is that the correction in China is more outspoken than in Europe or the US. It's likely that this trend will last for two or three years, in which companies and funds alike need to reposition themselves for the future, as funding is more difficult and budgets get tighter. The downturn also challenges the fundamentals of value creation and reveals major ecosystem gaps in China. At the same time government policies are pushing prices for innovative drugs down, which in turn decreases profits, and hurts investors' sentiments. Geopolitics also plays an increasing role, hurting prospects of Chinese companies to become global players. That being said, the long-term perspectives look good. The Chinese innovation ecosystem is showing signs of resilience, and Chinese biopharma companies are moving increasingly to real First-in-class drug development, hence slowly but steadily becoming globally competitive. A clear 'going global' trend is prevalent. The Chinese innovative pharma market is also still a growth story. McKinsey estimates it has room to grow to two and a half times the size of today.

The Biotech Winter Sets in, the Shortcomings Come Out

In 2021, putting money into a biotech seemed a pretty safe investment. The Covid-19 pandemic had put the biopharmaceutical industry in a positive spotlight, and IPOs were booming. All over the world biopharma was the way forward, while certain technologies in space were over-hyped. But the last two years have seen venture capital and overall funding dry up due to the economic downturn, which has heavily impacted many biotech companies.

Since 2022 the appetite for dealmaking and investing in biotech companies has decreased a lot, while venture capitalists hang onto their cash to survive and support their current portfolio companies. Big pharmaceutical companies are also being forced to cut back on R&D expenditures, which has effects for biotech companies as the smaller players depend on contracts with the major players. Without the prospects of deals with the big multinationals, investors are hesitant to fund biotechs even more.

Within this environment the Chinese biopharma sector is suffering even more than its US or European counterparts. In China, the biotech rollercoaster is more violent than in the US and Europe: the heights were higher, and the lows will be lower, especially as Chinese life sciences investors and biotechs experience their first industry downturn ever. As they are confronted with an unprecedented situation, they have also little experience in dealing with it. Many investors are financially too exposed, while they invested at extremely high valuations. Many portfolios will have zero return on investment or will even lose massive amounts of money. Some investors have been burned completely.

As McKinsey pointed out at the 2023 China Healthcare Summit, after a decade of rapid growth, which resulted in 60 listed companies and US$100+ billion market cap at its peak, China's biopharma innovation capital market is since mid-2021 is in a real reset mode. By the end of 2023, the market cap of two-thirds of the biotechs declined by 50% from its peak, erasing US$ 80 billion in market cap. Three-fourths of the biotechs are trading below IPO price. Some jewels of the industry like CStone Pharmaceuticals, are even reportedly facing bankruptcy. According to McKinsey the late-stage VC/PE funding has been hit especially hard. Within the last two years it has dropped 86% (compared to 13% in the US). Most China-originated biotechs are still not profitable. Of the 60 listed China-originated biotechs, more than 80% have revenue. But only eight biotechs (or 13%) are profitable. Because of the challenging funding environment, many biotechs are reducing their R&D burn rate, and halting development of assets which have limited chances for success.

The Chinese biopharma sector is undergoing a drastic reset. Old investment models are being changed, biotech companies need to focus on their core activities and save money where they can, while healthcare funds are looking to raise new money. All of this is under the current circumstances extremely tough. At the same time, some failures and shortcomings from the past are being exposed. As pointed out during the 2023 China Healthcare Summit there are several key points that need to be addressed. Despite all the enthusiasm and high-quality entrepreneurship, we saw during the boom years, it has become clear now that the caliber of Chinese biotech business and management leaders needs improvement. Real gaps exist between setting up a company, and the management capabilities and experience building a successful venture. Because of the relative inexperience of the management team, specifically the ability to make strategic decisions and to build a high-performance organization, are key issues. A new caliber of Chinese biotech leaders will need to step up. In the past too many companies focused on the same target, using the same modalities of technology. This led to fierce competition in a few MoAs—like GLP-1 or PD-1/PD-L1 inhibitors—and resulted in inefficient capital allocation. At the same time a lot of companies spent a lot of money on manufacturing facilities and rapidly expanding teams but invested too little in building depth in key functions to advance cutting-edge innovations. Another problem was the entrance of less experienced investors, the so-called 'dumb money', as opposed to 'smart money'. These investors have a very short-term mindset, and as such do not always make the right decision for the company. Classic examples are a fast-to-market approach and opportunistic clinical development approach, often with long-term negative consequences.

FDA Rejection of China Trials

Because of their limited international experience, China-originated biopharmas particularly face challenges in navigating overseas regulatory systems and institutions. Because they over-rely on CROs, Chinese biopharmas insufficiently understand the regulatory requirements in the US and Europe. Furthermore, they engage too late and reactive with the global expert network. Chinese companies need to provide clinical data that meet thresholds and standards that are already in place. Western regulators typically ask for patient populations that reflect their own region's demographics, which limits the value of China only trials.[1] Some FDA decisions to reject assets with exclusively Chinese data, certainly were an unexpected setback. Given the elaborate ecosystem of CROs, CDMOs and hospitals, investors have been betting on the idea that China could be used as a fast track to validate new drugs. As such they could get a faster ROI. In 2022 there were at least 25 applications from China in drug development phases, planned to be submitted or already under review by the FDA, which were predominantly or solely based on trial data from China.[2]

But also, in 2022 the FDA shattered the idea that it would approve Chinese drugs, purely based on Chinese clinical trials. Most notably was the non-approval of the Beigene-Eli Lily deal for Sintilimab, a PD-1 inhibitor lung cancer drug that was supposed to be a potential low-cost choice in a multibillion-dollar class. This drug was also a forerunner and poster boy deal for China-developed medicines that drew interest from Western big pharma. Two years earlier, Lilly paid a hefty US$ 200 million upfront and up to US$825 million in milestones for exclusive rights for Sintilimab, a drug that obtained China approval in 2018.[3] But

---

[1] McKinsey & Co. 2022. Vision 2028: How China could impact the global biopharma industry. https://www.mckinsey.com/~/media/mckinsey/industries/life%20sciences/our%20insights/vision%202028%20how%20china%20could%20impact%20the%20global%20biopharma%20industry/vision-2028-how-china-could-impact-the-global-biopharma-industry.pdf. Accessed on November 19, 2023.

[2] Reuters. 2022. U.S. FDA declines to approve two more China-tested drugs. www.reuters.com/business/healthcare-pharmaceuticals/us-fda-declines-approve-hutchmeds-china-tested-cancer-drug-2022-05-02/. Accessed on October 29, 2023.

[3] Fiercepharma. 2022. Eli Lilly dumps Innovent PD-a after FDA rebuff, nixing high-profile Chinese cancer drug. https://www.fiercepharma.com/pharma/eli-lilly-dumps-innovents-pd-1-after-fda-rebuff-nixing-poster-child-china-developed-cancer. Accessed on October 28, 2023.

the fact that the drug only had undergone clinical trials in China, was not convincing enough for the FDA to get approval in the US. BeiGene was not the only company which encountered this setback. A Hutchmed anti-cancer drug met the same problem, despite the fact it had carried out two phase 3 trials in China and one bridging study in the US.[4] A drug developed by Junshi Biosciences met the same fate. It also got rejected by the FDA which recommended a multi-regional trial.[5]

Another challenge for China-originated biopharmas revolves around data and rigor. The clinical practices and trial data of China-originated biotechs must fully meet the FDA and EMEA's requirements on data disclosure and data security.[6]

It's clear that a pathway for future applications will have to be focused on multiregional clinical trials and clear data generation. And even then, there are doubts about what regions are deemed to be sufficiently valid to carry out clinical trials. The FDA hinted that clinical trials conducted in Africa and South America need 'strengthening'. They explained that this was due to these regions being currently underrepresented in oncology multiregional clinical trials and would boost diversity, thereby increasing the representation of racial and ethnic minorities.[7] With many treatments already progressing through an application in the US, the question will be whether companies now pivot to establish multiregional trials, which will undoubtedly increase the costs. In order to avoid these issues and get clarity om how to get their product approved in the US, Chinese drug manufacturers should engage with the FDA early and formally to work

[4] ThinkChina. 2023. Cancelled contracts upset Chinese drugmakers' overseas push. www.thinkchina.sg/cancelled-contracts-upset-chinese-drugmakers-overseas-push. Accessed on October 29, 2023.

[5] Reuters. 2022. U.S. FDA declines to approve two more China-tested drugs. www.reuters.com/business/healthcare-pharmaceuticals/us-fda-declines-approve-hutchmeds-china-tested-cancer-drug-2022-05-02/. Accessed on October 29, 2023.

[6] McKinsey & Co. 2022. Vision 2028: How China could impact the global biopharma industry. https://www.mckinsey.com/~/media/mckinsey/industries/life%20sciences/our%20insights/vision%202028%20how%20china%20could%20impact%20the%20global%20biopharma%20industry/vision-2028-how-china-could-impact-the-global-biopharma-industry.pdf. Accessed on November 19, 2023.

[7] Pharmaphorum. 2022. FDA's treatment of China developed drugs spurs demand for multiregional clinical trials. https://pharmaphorum.com/market-access-2/fdas-treatment-of-china-developed-drugs-spurs-demands. Accessed on November 21, 2023.

out these nuances and gain upfront guidance. This is particularly important in the innovative oncology area where 15% of Chinese firms are already running international multicenter trials.[8]

Partnerships Get Canceled

The route of internationalization via out-licensing drugs can be lucrative. At the same time it can also be precarious, with multiple contracts terminated over the last years. In 2023 alone multiple partnerships with Chinese biopharma companies were terminated. Jacobio Pharmaceuticals, I-Mab, BeiGene and Innovent, have had collaborations terminated by foreign buyers of their product's rights. Abbvie returned the global rights to Jacobio Pharmaceuticals' SHP2 inhibitors, which were in clinical trial phase worldwide. Abbvie also terminated a 2020 deal to co-develop and market I-Mab's lead cancer drug candidate lemzoparlimab. AbbVie previously acquired the rights to different I-Mab's antibody-based drug candidates, outside China for US$180 million upfront payment and an additional US$1.74 billion in milestone payments.[9] In the space of two months Novartis ended two partnership deals with BeiGene. One of them was the US$650 million upfront licensing deal for a PD-1 inhibitor, where Novartis obtained co-development and co-commercialization rights to the drug for North America, Japan, the EU and several other countries.

Since 2018 at least ten such out-licensing agreements have been cancelled.[10] While the financial impact on bigger companies like Beigene is of course big, smaller startups take the hardest hit as they usually have only one or two core assets and will find it almost impossible to find new collaboration partners after experiencing a return.

---

[8] Reuters. 2022. U.S. FDA advisers call for new trial of Lilly, Innovent lung cancer drug. www.reuters.com/business/healthcare-pharmaceuticals/us-fda-panel-discuss-lung-cancer-drug-tested-only-china-2022-02-10/. Accessed on November 22, 2023.

[9] Reuters. 2023. Abbvie terminates deal with I-Mab to develop cancer drug. https://www.reuters.com/markets/deals/abbvie-terminates-deal-with-i-mab-develop-cancer-drug-2023-09-22/. Accessed on November 18, 2023.

[10] ThinkChina. 2023. Cancelled contracts upset Chinese drugmakers' overseas push. www.thinkchina.sg/cancelled-contracts-upset-chinese-drugmakers-overseas-push. Accessed on October 29, 2023.

The reasons for these recent returns of out-licensed assets by MNCs are not always clear. The fact that international cooperations are being cancelled is not unusual in the biopharma sector. Disappointing data, bad market conditions or a change of corporate strategy are all reasons often cited. Novartis said a changing PD-1 inhibitor landscape led to the decision to terminate the agreements with Beigene. Back in 2019, Celgene returned another drug to BeiGene in the middle of its US$74 billion merger with Bristol Myers Squibb (BMS) because of a conflict of interest with an asset from BMS.[11] Just like the case of BeiGene and Novartis, other global pharmaceutical companies like Roche, MSD and Bristol-Myers Squibb all faced problems in the research and clinical trials of their TIGIT inhibitors and stopped the development. So, this seems to indicate that Novartis decided to stop the cooperation with BeiGene because of broadly encountered scientific issues. The problem however is that in most cases the companies involved didn't publicly state the reason why global or regional rights are returned, which leads to speculation about whether the termination was related to problems with the drugs themselves. This in turn questions then the quality of the Chinese drug discovery and impacts the whole Chinese biopharma sector.

IPOs Are Getting More Difficult

In August 2023 the Securities Regulatory Commission (CSRC) announced a series of policies and new measures to boost the Chinese stock market. The new policies were designed to raise the bar for companies to IPO. In 2022 China was the world's busiest IPO market, eclipsing Hong Kong and the US, as hi-tech companies were encouraged to raise money from the stock market to support China's technology self-sufficiency drive. That year about 422 companies raised US$80.9 billion from IPOs on mainland exchanges.[12] But 2023 saw a wave of sell-offs, hence the intervention from the CSRC. Among others it pledged to

---

[11] FiercePharma. 2023. After TIGIT divorce, Novartis returns tislelizumab to BeiGene as PD-1 gains first European nod. https://www.fiercepharma.com/pharma/after-tigit-divorce-novartis-returns-tislelizumab-beigene-pd-1-gains-first-european-nod. Accessed on November 18, 2023.

[12] South China Morning Post. 2023. Why China is restricting IPOs to drive up US$9.7 trillion onshore stock market. https://www.scmp.com/business/china-business/article/3234258/why-china-restricting-ipos-drive-us97-trillion-onshore-stock-market. Accessed on September 14, 2023.

restrict new share sales. These measures are nothing now as administrative control over IPOs is a conventional tool used by the Chinese securities regulator to prop up the market. It happened for instance in 2015 when IPOs were halted for several months to stop the wave of sell-offs that erased trillions of dollars. During the global financial crisis in 2008, the CSRC also imposed a ten-month moratorium on new share sales.[13]

From the perspective of pharmaceutical investment, these measures however profoundly rewrite the logic of the primary and secondary markets of the pharmaceutical industry for a long time to come, especially for unprofitable biotech companies. Among others, the new policies stipulate that shareholders cannot reduce the amount of shares they hold via the secondary market, in case the company doesn't meet stringent financial requirements. As by far most listed biotech companies are not profitable—and won't be for years to come—, this has severe sequences. Investors now will think twice before investing in the biotech sector as the exit potential has been reduced significantly. In the biotech sector IPOs are typically the main way for venture capitalists to exit the companies they invested in. Furthermore, listed and cash-rich biotech companies will be cautious in spending money on R&D or further development of their pipeline, as this eats away their cash. The more cash they burn, the worse the cash position, the more difficult it is to meet the government requirements to remain listed, so the higher the risk for shareholders that they cannot sell their shares. Consequently, they rather will spend their money on late-stage assets, which require much less early-stage R&D. Another result is that, as IPOs will become rare, the number of mergers and acquisitions (M&A) will probably increase. Until now and despite the fact that there are hundreds of biotechs in China, M&A cases were rare in the sector. That might change now, as investors will look for different and more pragmatic exit options, besides an IPO.

---

[13] South China Morning Post. 2023. Why China is restricting IPOs to drive up US$9.7 trillion onshore stock market. https://www.scmp.com/business/china-business/article/3234258/why-china-restricting-ipos-drive-us97-trillion-onshore-stock-market. Accessed on September 14, 2023.

Common Prosperity and Health Economics Are Here to Stay

Besides the global downturn which hurt the biopharma sector worldwide, and the shortcomings of Chinese biopharma companies, companies in China are facing an extra set of unique challenges. One of them is the government policy of 'Common prosperity', which since a few years now, has become the new mantra. A barrage of regulations has supported this goal, targeting high-growth business segments, among which is the healthcare sector. A major problem for the sector is the increasing financial drain on China's public healthcare system and other public services. Furthermore, slowing economic growth will have real implications on government healthcare spending, especially when we are talking about the disease burden. The example of diabetes shows the problem. In 2021 there were an estimated 141 million diabetics in the country, a tenth of the population, and the highest level globally.[14] Between 2020 and 2030 the total costs of diabetes are estimated to increase from US$250.2 billion to US$460.4 billion, corresponding to an annual growth rate of 6.32%. The total costs of diabetes as a percentage of GDP however would increase from 1.58% to 1.69%, suggesting a faster growth in the economic burden of diabetes than China's economic growth.[15]

The financial burden on the healthcare system became even more apparent during the COVID-19 pandemic. Up to the end of 2022 China enforced a rigorous zero-tolerance policy with mass PCR testing, lockdowns and other pandemic control measures which consequently started to take its financial toll. In 2022 according to annual budget reports from local governments, Chinese provinces spent a whopping US$51.6 billion on Covid-19 containment measures. That year China's biggest provincial economy, Guangdong, spent around US$10 billion, including vaccinations, PCR testing for its citizens and subsidies for medical staff. That number was up 56.8% from COVID-related spending in 2021 and

---

[14] World Economic Forum. 2023. How medical technology is tackling China's diabetes crisis. www.weforum.org/agenda/2023/06/diabetes-china-medical-technology/. Accessed on November 3, 2023.

[15] National Library of Medicine. 2023. Projected rapid growth in diabetes disease burden and economic burden in China: A spatio-temporal study from 2020 to 2030. https://pubmed.ncbi.nlm.nih.gov/36817869/. Accessed on November 3, 2023.

more than doubled the 2020 spending.[16] One of the consequences was that after years of enforcing a very costly zero-Covid policy, the Chinese government—strapped of cash—started to cut medical benefits, as part of a national overhaul mainly intended to cover deficits in public medical insurance funds.[17]

One thing however is sure: China will not let the costs of the healthcare system spiral out of control. It will keep reducing drug prices, using several strategies such as VBP, and increased competitive national and local tendering. Health technology assessment (HTA) is also a significant part of these policies. HTA is a systematic and multidisciplinary evaluation of the properties of health technologies and interventions that aims to determine the value of a health technology and to provide guidance on how these technologies can be used in health systems around the world.[18] In China HTA is being used to assess funding for innovative medicines with an uncertain long-term benefit and how to structure insurance reimbursement of these drugs. It's also being used to allow drugs on the NRDL, and in RWE.[19] For the pharma sector it means that drug reimbursements will be aligned more closely with approaches widely used in Europe in terms of health economics and pricing. China will shy away from a U.S.-style healthcare system with its out-of-control spiraling costs.

For the pharma companies this simply means increased financial pressure. Profit margins at China's pharma companies are already shrinking under the pressures of high expenditure on R&D, procurement and dropping prices. Price cuts of 40% to 50% for innovative drugs and 80 to 90% for generic drugs have become the norm now.[20] The

---

[16] Reuters. 2022. Chinese provinces spent at least $51.6 billion on COVOD curbs in 2022. www.reuters.com/world/china/chinese-provinces-spent-least-516-billion-covid-curbs-2022-2023-02-15/. Accessed on September 8, 2023.

[17] CNN. 2023. Chinese cities are so broke, cutting medical benefits for seniors. https://edition.cnn.com/2023/03/31/economy/china-pension-protests-aging-society-intl-hnk/index.html. Accessed on September 8, 2023.

[18] World Health Organization. 2023. Health Technology Assessment. https://www.who.int/health-topics/health-technology-assessment#tab=tab_1. Accessed on November 21, 2023.

[19] BMJ. 2023 Health technology assessment in China. https://www.bmj.com/hta-in-china. Accessed on November 21, 2023.

[20] National Library of Medicine. 2023. Successes and challenges of China's health care reform: a four-decade perspective spanning 1985–2023. www.ncbi.nlm.nih.gov/pmc/articles/PMC10469830/. Accessed on November 21, 2023.

drug procurement system hurts hospitals also. Hospitals used to be able to charge markups on pharmaceutical products. These drug sales were fundamental to hospitals' ability to turn a profit. In 2012 the revenue from drug sales accounted for 44.3% of the total revenue of public hospitals, but after the procurement reforms of 2020, this proportion dropped to 30.6%. Much of the debt of China's hospitals is owed to drug companies.[21] As a result, all hospitals are suffering, something that was made worse by the Covid-19 pandemic which reduced the flow of clientele to hospitals, drastically reducing their revenues and profits. Between the start of the epidemic in 2020 and the end in 2022, more than 2,000 private hospitals have gone bankrupt.[22]

President Xi Jinping 'common prosperity' campaign is also visible in its graft busting. In China, anti-corruption campaigns have been launched since 2012, and drugmakers were caught in the crossfire before. The reasons were simple. In the past China's health system was widely criticized for its lack of unaffordable drugs. At the time, public hospitals used the 15% drug price-adding policy to increase hospital revenues, and doctors were motivated -and often bribed- to prescribe high-priced and unnecessary drugs to patients. Because of this practice GSK for instance was fined a US$489 million in 2014.[23] Patients and their families on the other hand, however, were overwhelmed by huge drug expenditures or even pushed back into poverty because of illness, which gradually aroused wide concern among the public and the government.

It was, however, only recently again that the healthcare system was targeted. In Summer 2023 an anti-corruption campaign was launched in the healthcare sector, which has been described as the biggest crackdown on corruption in the history of the industry. At least 177 hospital bosses and Chinese Communist party (CCP) secretaries had been placed

---

[21] The China Project. 2022. Why China's hospitals are going out of business in the middle of a pandemic. https://thechinaproject.com/2022/12/06/why-chinas-hospitals-are-going-out-of-business-in-the-middle-of-a-pandemic/. Accessed on November 19, 2023.

[22] The China Project. 2022. Why China's hospitals are going out of business in the middle of a pandemic. https://thechinaproject.com/2022/12/06/why-chinas-hospitals-are-going-out-of-business-in-the-middle-of-a-pandemic/. Accessed on November 19, 2023.

[23] Reuters. China hands drug maker GSK record $489 million fine for paying bribes. https://www.reuters.com/article/us-gsk-china-idUSKBN0HE0TC20140919/. Accessed on November 24, 2023.

under investigation. They were accused to use their position to procure kickbacks when purchasing medical equipment and medicines.[24] This campaign in the pharmaceutical sector is in fact aimed at rooting out corruption in the whole medical supply chain, including medical institutions and funds. Research shows that many Chinese consider doctors as one of the most corrupt professionals in China. The perception among many Chinese is that doctors must be paid bribes to speed up medical consultations, and that hospitals charge exorbitant prices for medicines. At the same time research also shows that those paying the bribes are often pharmaceutical and medical equipment suppliers.[25]

The short-term consequences were predictable. Shares of stock-listed drugmakers dropped immediately as investors worried about the anti-corruption campaign potentially hurting sales figures. In July 2023 the CSI medical services index, which tracks China's largest listed pharmaceutical companies on the Shenzhen stock exchange, dropped over 5%. In the same month drugmakers Rongsheng Biotech Co, and Fujian Mindong Rejuvenation Pharmaceutical Co. withdrew their IPO application, after regulators started to ask questions about their sales promotion activities and sales expenses. In addition, as the National Health Commission of China has proclaimed that some academic events are used as a channel to bribe doctors, in August 2023 at least ten academic conferences were postponed.[26]

It's clear that Beijing will crack down on any sector seen as increasing people's economic burden. The underlying principle is that healthcare is like a social service that should principally be in state hands. It's the state's job to guarantee a level of provision of basic services, whether it's education or healthcare. Therefore it's important for the state to play

---

[24] The Guardian. 2023. China renews crackdown on corruption in healthcare. www.theguardian.com/world/2023/aug/17/china-renews-crackdown-on-corruption-in-health care. Accessed on September 8, 2023.

[25] National Library of Medicine. 2021. The changing forms of corruption in China. Bakken and Wang. www.ncbi.nlm.nih.gov/pmc/articles/PMC8076439/. Accessed September 8, 2023.

[26] Reuters. 2023. China drugmakers axe IPO plans as they face scrutiny in anti-graft drive. www.reuters.com/world/china/china-drugmakers-axe-ipo-plans-they-face-scrutiny-anti-graft-drive-2023-08-11. Accessed September 8, 2023.

a (key) role in the healthcare sector.[27] As a result, the government is creating a more limited sandbox for the private sector to play in. Basically, the message from the government is that the private sector should be doing innovation as a national service, as opposed to doing innovation for profitability goals only.

NRDL FORCES TORWARD AFFORDABLE INNOVATION

As China has embarked on a policy of providing good quality medicines at very affordable prices, western pharmaceutical companies and Chinese companies alike need to rethink their China strategy and analyze how their drugs fit into the Chinese market. This environment is a catalyst for companies to transform their China strategy and perhaps even their global strategy. The concept of affordable innovation will be key.

For Chinese biopharma companies obviously the first market that must work is the Chinese market itself. As most bigger and smaller Chinese biopharma companies don't have global potential, their drugs might only be approved in China, and as such the only revenue stream they can enjoy, is the Chinese market. For them, the Chinese market can work in three ways. Firstly, the demand for a drug can be so high that patients are willing to pay for it out of pocket. Secondly, the drug can be covered by commercial health insurance plans. Thirdly, and arguably most importantly, the drug can be added to the NRDL.[28]

For patients and companies, the NRDL is at the same time a blessing and a curse. China is now updating the NRDL annually, which is good news. The list is also continuously improved and NRDL listings are faster than ever. The NRDL also has proven to be beneficial for patients as they receive much faster treatment now with new medicines. But there is also a downside. For patients who suffer from a rare disease however, the NRDL is a barrier to get access to the newest drugs. Companies which focus on rare diseases -an increasing priority of global portfolios- face an

---

[27] Reuters. 2023. China's crackdowns rewrite investors' private sector playbook. https://www.reuters.com/markets/asia/chinas-crackdowns-rewrite-investors-private-sector-playbook-2023-08-17/. Accessed on November 21, 2023.

[28] McKinsey & Co. 2022. Vision 2028: How China could impact the global biopharma industry. https://www.mckinsey.com/~/media/mckinsey/industries/life%20sciences/our%20insights/vision%202028%20how%20china%20could%20impact%20the%20global%20biopharma%20industry/vision-2028-how-china-could-impact-the-global-biopharma-industry.pdf. Accessed on November 19, 2023.

uphill battle in China as severe price cuts are necessary to make it on the NRDL. In 2020 and 2021, seven orphan drugs were included in the NRDL. However, the prices of the reimbursed products didn't even come close to their prices in other countries, and a substantial level of discount is necessary to be included. In 2022 NRDL a 94% price cut was even needed to make the list.[29] This in turn means that many companies will not consider China as a market to launch orphan drugs, which eventually hurts the patients.

To get listed on the NRDL, price cuts have become the norm. Since price negotiations were formally introduced, drugmakers needed to offer a 50% discount in order to get their drugs accepted on the list.[30] It's also not easy to get on the list, even with the necessary discounts. In 2020, 704 drugs passed the initial review, but only 162 were shortlisted for negotiation, of which 119 products were successfully accepted, giving an overall success rate of 17%.[31] In 2022, 111 new drugs entered the NRDL with an average price cut reaching 60.1%, which is close to the 2021 figure of 61.7%.[32] Among the 2022 newly added drugs, 56 are for chronic diseases (diabetes, hypertension, psychoactive disease, etc.), 23 for tumor, 17 for anti-infection, and seven for rare diseases. The adjusted 2022 NRDL covered 2,967 drugs, including 1,586 Western (chemical/biological) drugs and 1,381 Chinese patent medicines.[33]

---

[29] GreenbergTraurig. 2023. China on the move: Lesson from China's national negotiation of drug prices in 2022. www.gtlaw.com/en/insights/2023/2/china-on-the-move-lesson-from-chinas-national-negotiation-of-drug-prices-in-2022. Accessed on September 20, 2023.

[30] Thomson Reuters Practical Law. 2023. Life Sciences commercialization in China: Overview. https://uk.practicallaw.thomsonreuters.com/0-568-3025?transitionType=Default&contextData=(sc.Default)&firstPage=true#co_anchor_a396730. Accessed on November 4, 2023.

[31] National Library of Medicine. 2023.Access to innovative drugs and the National Reimbursement Drug List in China: Changing dynamics and future trends in pricing and reimbursement. www.ncbi.nlm.nih.gov/pmc/articles/PMC10266112/. Accessed on September 20, 2023.

[32] GreenbergTraurig. 2023. China on the move: Lesson from China's national negotiation of drug prices in 2022. www.gtlaw.com/en/insights/2023/2/china-on-the-move-lesson-from-chinas-national-negotiation-of-drug-prices-in-2022. Accessed on September 20, 2023.

[33] Baipharm. 2023. China published the preliminary list of drugs for 2023 National Drugs Reimbursement List (NDRL). https://baipharm.chemlinked.com/news/china-adds-111-drugs-to-2022-national-reimbursement-drug-list. Accessed on September 20, 2023.

China's NRDL Negotiations

Year	Number of Drugs for Negotiation	Number of Drugs Added to NRDL + Drugs Staying in NRDL via Contract Renewal	Average Price Cut	Contract Term
2015 (pilot)	5	3	58.6%	Procurement term within 2016-2017
2017	44	36	39%	2018/01/01-2019/12/31
2018	18	17	56.7%	2019/01/01-2020/12/31
2019	150 (119+31)	97 (70+27)	60.7%+26.4%	2020/01/01-2021/12/31
2020	162	119	50.64%	2021/03/01-2022/12/31
2021	117	94 (67+27)	61.71%	2022/01/01-2022/12/31
2022	147	121 (108+13)	60.1%	Starting from 2023/03/01 (Starting from 2023/04/01 for Azvudine and Qingfei Paidu Granules)

Source Baipharm. 2023. China published the preliminary list of drugs for 2023 National Drug Reimbursement List (NDRL)

The NRDL and its negotiation scheme have also not favored MNCs. First-in-class products or the first product for a specific unmet are not easily included in NRDL, with the exception that other alternative products or close follower drug candidates would become available soon after.[34] At the beginning Western drug makers dominated the list. In 2017, out of the 36 drugs on the NRDL Category B list, 31 were Western originated for various indications including cancers, rare diseases, cardiovascular diseases and diabetes.[35] But as China-originated innovative medicines got approved, competition increased. Now in the oncology space Chinese companies dominate the list. In 2022 oncology drugs from Innovent, Hengrui, Junshi, Beigene, JW Therapeutics and Fosun Kite

---

[34] GreenbergTraurig. 2023. China on the move: Lesson from China's national negotiation of drug prices in 2022. www.gtlaw.com/en/insights/2023/2/china-on-the-move-lesson-from-chinas-national-negotiation-of-drug-prices-in-2022. Accessed on September 20, 2023.

[35] National Library of Medicine. 2023. Access to innovative drugs and the National Reimbursement Drug List in China: Changing dynamics and future trends in pricing and reimbursement. www.ncbi.nlm.nih.gov/pmc/articles/PMC10266112/. Accessed on September 20, 2023.

all got included on the list. Only multinational pharmaceutical companies like Pfizer and Takeda succeeded in getting their anti-cancer drugs included in the 2022 NRDL.[36]

This means that the innovative drugs of multinational pharmaceutical companies in China, are losing their edge. Not only is the patent-related marketing exclusivity of their products ending, but increasingly Chinese biopharma companies are also competing head on with their innovative medicines. More generic drugs and biosimilars made by Chinese domestic companies are joining the competition. Moreover, by following a strategy of affordable innovation, Chinese biopharma companies are very much willing to offer cheaper drugs to get approved to the NRDL list. Foreign drugmakers thus increasingly face price pressure. In fact, because of NRDL system and the significant price cuts it requires, foreign companies become hesitant to commercialize their most innovative drugs in China.[37] Only 25% of drugs approved by the FDA in the last five years are available in China, reflecting the limited business interest and value to global biopharma.[38] Domestic manufacturers have been willing to accept very low prices to get access to the NRDL, while multinationals often cease negotiations because domestic firms have driven the price down to a level where it is no longer financially appealing for them to compete. In this way Chinese firms are blocking access to Western companies.

This was notably visible in the PD-1/PD-L1 inhibitor space. Keytruda (Merck), Opdivo (BMS), Imfinzi (AstraZeneca) and Tecentriq (Roche) have had successful commercialization in Western markets but have all been blocked from NRDL listing by domestically developed products.[39] For PD-(L)1 drugs, the top local brands treat most of the patients,

---

[36] GreenbergTraurig. 2023. China on the move: Lesson from China's national negotiation of drug prices in 2022. www.gtlaw.com/en/insights/2023/2/china-on-the-move-lesson-from-chinas-national-negotiation-of-drug-prices-in-2022. Accessed on September 20, 2023.

[37] National Library of Medicine. 2023. Successes and challenges of China's health care reform: a four-decade perspective spanning 1985–2023. www.ncbi.nlm.nih.gov/pmc/articles/PMC10469830/. Accessed on November 21, 2023.

[38] Harri Jarvelainen. 2023. Key takeaways from the McKinsey China Biopharma report 2023—Growing pains and more. https://www.linkedin.com/pulse/key-takeaways-from-mckinsey-china-biopharma-report-harri-3rf3c. Accessed on November 22, 2023.

[39] Windrose Consulting Group. 2023. China market access through cross-border partnership: Opportunities and challenges for western pharmaceuticals. https://windrosecg.com/posts/chinese-market-healthcare. Accessed on October 26, 2023.

while the MNC brands are being largely left out. Therefore, in order to get accepted on the NRDL, foreign drug manufacturers need to find other ways in. Partnerships offer alternatives. Novartis, AstraZeneca and Pfizer succesfully concluded joint commercialization deals for local PD-1/PD-L1s.[40] This means that in fields where Chinese companies can compete head on, the best way forward for an MNC is a collaboration with a domestic player. Besides the PD-1/PD-L1 inhibitor space, arguably the next sector where Western companies will face fierce competition is the ADC field. Domestically produced Aidixi from RemeGen was the first ADC to be NRDL listed in 2021 after accepting a discount of more than 70%. This discount is more than likely to set the bar for follow-on ADC NRDL negotiations with both foreign and domestic firms.[41]

Because of its price cuts, one of the major criticisms of the NRDL is that domestic innovation is not receiving sufficient financial reward. Domestic drugs such as PD-(L)1s, have brought a lot of patient value (20 times lower out-of-pocket costs of local PD-1s compared to imported products), but the value for the biopharma companies has been below expectations.

Most industry experts express their concern about the sustainability of the market access environment to support innovation. Only five China-originated innovative drugs now have over US$200 million domestic sales.[42] This means the rewards for innovation are not yet sufficient to warrant the increased R&D investments by local biotech companies. This remains a counterweight to what might otherwise be the positive effects of the NRDL's expansion. Strong price control policies could hinder the development of innovative drugs in the domestic market, in particular

---

[40] Windrose Consulting Group. 2023. China market access through cross-border partnership: Opportunities and challenges for western pharmaceuticals. https://windrosecg.com/posts/chinese-market-healthcare. Accessed on October 26, 2023.

[41] Windrose Consulting Group. 2023. China market access through cross-border partnership: opportunities and challenges for western pharmaceuticals. https://windrosecg.com/posts/chinese-market-healthcare. Accessed on October 26, 2023.

[42] Harri Jarvelainen. 2023. Key takeaways from the McKinsey China Biopharma report 2023—growing pains and more. https://www.linkedin.com/pulse/key-takeaways-from-mckinsey-china-biopharma-report-harri-3rf3c. Accessed on November 22, 2023.

the first-in-class drugs.[43] Some people in the industry go even so far to say that the pricing policies might kill any innovation. The result is that although there is tangible progress in access to innovation, the pace is slower than what is needed for sustained growth. Because of these restrictions, it's possible China will face big hurdles in developing really innovate breakthrough technologies. Therefore, the sustainability of the Chinese pharmaceutical system remains an issue.

To keep their advantage locally, foreign companies should develop more innovative pharmaceuticals to meet the clinical needs in China. If the increase in sales volume can offset the price cuts, foreign companies can also increase their competitiveness by getting products included in the NRDL. In 2021 AstraZeneca was the largest foreign pharma company in China. Its US$5.99 billion sales in China were heavily related to volume-based procurement and the NRDL.[44] Trade-off between profitability and sale will be a major product launch decision for each company to make in the next decade, in light of the structural constraints of the Chinese market and a clearer healthcare policy agenda. At the same time MNCs can also enrich their global portfolio with local innovative assets/technology platforms. They can also explore innovating global business model with China as a testing ground for new assets. Chinese investors are still keen to set up joint ventures in China with foreign drugmakers.

Protectionist Policies

While China is gradually reducing market access barriers in many sectors, at the same time it also embarks on protectionist policies and sets up import restrictions in areas of high strategic importance. This is also true for the healthcare sector. In the medtech space China's government has already implemented new rules to reduce the high dependency on imports. According to reports, about two-thirds of Chinese medical devices used by local hospitals and clinics are imported from Western groups. China's localization policy however aims to reverse that

---

[43] National Library of Medicine. 2023. Successes and challenges of China's health care reform: A four-decade perspective spanning 1985–2023. www.ncbi.nlm.nih.gov/pmc/articles/PMC10469830/. Accessed on November 21, 2023.

[44] Baipharm 2022. Multinational pharma companies record sales growth in 2021. https://baipharm.chemlinked.com/news/multinational-pharma-companies-record-sales-growth-in-2021. Accessed on November 24, 2023.

number by requiring domestic industry players to supply 70% of these medical devices by 2025.[45] In practice this is however not always so easy to achieve, as Western companies keep upgrading their products and launching technologically superior models. But the policies goals are clear and aim to spur domestic companies to innovate more. China's government is pushing for domestic technology breakthroughs in medtech, hoping to move China's medical device sector up the value chain. With this type of policy support, domestic medtech companies are expanding into the medium and high-end market via partnerships or acquisitions.[46] Western companies from their side can only secure market share in China by further localization of production and partnerships.

The biotech sector has not been touched yet, but that most likely is only a matter of time. China traditionally uses a three-stage playbook to build up a certain high-tech industry into a global force to be reckoned with. Phase one starts with allowing foreign imports. Phase two transitions to requiring and incenting foreign production in China and encourages technology transfer. As a final stage the policies usually switch to supporting China's domestic firms. In the biopharma sector China is active in phase one and two. Chinese government policies are supportive of inbound foreign direct investment (FDI), and the biotech industry is on the encouraged list of the Chinese government's Catalog of Industries for guiding foreign investment. And while the sector is open to 100% ownership of foreign facilities, there are incentives to form joint ventures which often use technology from abroad. Until now it seems China's regulators have expressed less interest in protectionism of domestic companies. It now sees its role as providing the public with safer and more efficacious medicines regardless of who makes them. That however might change as soon as China has built enough biotech companies which can compete with its foreign competitors.

---

[45] Reuters. 2023. West's latest corporate risk: Medical graft. www.reuters.com/breakingviews/wests-latest-china-corporate-risk-medical-graft-2023-10-23/. Accessed on November 3, 2023.

[46] Tablechina. 2022. Market for medical technology becomes more local. https://table.media/china/en/sinolytics-radar-en/market-for-medical-technology-becomes-more-local/. Accessed on November 3, 2023.

De-risking in the Emerging US-China Biotech War

Over the last years political tensions between the US, the current superpower and China, a growing superpower, have intensified. China is looking for its rightful place in the global world order, while the US is defending it. This of course creates tensions which are being played out politically, economically and ideologically. The US and China are not only waging a trade war with each other, but also increasingly a financial and technology war. Both countries are competing in research and development, believing that technological hegemony in a wide range of fields will determine not only economic, but also security superiority. US efforts to restrict licensing of technology date back from 2018 when the Department of Commerce earmarked several technologies for potential export controls from. It also expanded the powers of the Committee on Foreign Investment in the United States (CFIUS) to review foreign investments and acquisitions that may impact national security.[47] This has set up the legal architecture to close off US industrial assets to Chinese access, most notable to been seen in the chip export restrictions. They were designed to preserve the US' relative advantage against other countries in tech-driven industries.

Despite the Department of Commerce in 2018 explicitly suggesting biotech as a critical technology, the sector hasn't been affected heavily yet. But tensions are rising. Despite the obvious commercial potential between the US and Chinese biopharma sectors, biotechnology is becoming the latest strategic sector in the US-China technology competition. It seems to become now a particular field of focus as biotech can be utilized in pharmaceuticals and regenerative medicine. Because of this it has the possibility to become the key to energy, food and national security.

In 2022 the US accelerated its efforts in promoting the development of biotechnology as part of its national security policy. US President Joe Biden signed an executive order on expanding investment in biotechnology and boost manufacturing in the domestic biotech sector.[48] This

---

[47] World Bio Market Insights. 2022. The US-China tech war: Will biotech be next?. https://worldbiomarketinsights.com/the-us-china-tech-war-will-biotech-be-next/. Accessed on November 22, 2023.

[48] The Japan News. 2023. Future world order: Economic tug-of-war / biotech serves as next front of U.S China tensions. https://japannews.yomiuri.co.jp/politics/political-series/20230108-82686/. Accessed on November 22, 2023.

National Biotechnology and Biomanufacturing Initiative (NBBI) aims to expand US biotechnology innovation and production capacity further in order to extend its absolute global lead in these fields.[49] The government also released a plan for creating a safe and secure bioeconomy—meaning safeguarding biological data—, while commissioning new studies of security risks and the biomanufacturing supply chain.[50] President Biden himself stated that the actions taken are going to ensure that America leads the world in biotechnology and biomanufacturing, so that the US does not have to rely on anybody else in the world. China is already the largest global supplier of active pharmaceutical ingredients, a point that has raised concerns during the pandemic given rising geopolitical tensions and policies promoting domestic protectionism.[51] At the same the US government stressed again the importance of preventing the outflow of biotech technology to China.[52] Therefore, the US has embarked on a two-pronged strategy. On the one hand, the US is building up capacity and stamping down competitors. Here is in fact copies the Chinese game plan as it matches the support that the Chinese government has been throwing at its own bioeconomy for years. On the other hand, the US has also the legal tools in hand to restrict foreign investments in the biosector, and controlling exports when needed. One of the first victims was Wuxi Biologics. In 2022 the US government added the company to its 'unverified list'. While this does not prevent American companies from doing business with the firm, it adds procedures and paperwork. In 2023 Wuxi Biologics was removed from the list.

One specific area which is already affected, is the gene-editing field. Gene-editing technologies have become more precise and vastly cheaper, making it easier to reprogram organisms. At the same time, it's long been

---

[49] World Bio Market Insights. 2022. The US-China tech war: will biotech be next? https://worldbiomarketinsights.com/the-us-china-tech-war-will-biotech-be-next/. Accessed on November 22, 2023.

[50] Financial Times. 2023. There is a new US national security obsession—Biotech. https://www.ft.com/content/cb9cd845-e9b0-4243-97f3-c315dac11fb4. Accessed on November 22, 2023.

[51] Capital Group. 2020. China's biopharma industry moves closer to inflection point. https://www.capitalgroup.com/institutional/insights/articles/china-biopharma-stocks.html. Accessed on November 4, 2023.

[52] The Japan News. 2023. Future world order: Economic tug-of-war / biotech serves as next front of U.S China tensions. https://japannews.yomiuri.co.jp/politics/political-series/20230108-82686/. Accessed on November 22, 2023.

recognized that DNA is just a complex type of code, telling cells how to operate. When applying massive volumes of computing power to DNA, it can be used for military purposes.[53] It has for instance the potential to create viruses to target specific ethic groups, making it a threat to the national security of any country. Because of this, the BGI Group, the most famous Chinese genetic sequencing firm was in 2023 added to the US 'Entity List' which restricts technology transfers and makes it hard for them to receive shipments of US goods from suppliers.[54] The primary justification for this action was that the company had been 'contributing to monitoring and surveillance', including of ethnic minorities in China. But the new regulations also state that BGI's programs of 'collection and analysis of genetic data present a significant risk of diversion to China's military'.[55] The latter was probably the real reason.

China from its side, has also taken measures to protect its gene-editing field. Here the catalyst was the ethical scandal in 2018 when Chinese researcher He Jiankui utilized CRISPR-Cas9 gene editing to change the DNA of the embryos of seven couples. This was met by global condemnation and a global moratorium on gene-editing embryos.[56] In China also there was an outcry and some soul-searching on the part of researchers, institutions and governments on how to handle genetic research, materials and data. In 2022 Chinese regulators tightened the bioethics regulations related to human genetics. The new regulations define human genetic resources as genetic materials, including organs, tissues and cells, as well as genetic information, such as the human genome and genes. The guidelines also state that organizations and individuals outside of China, as well as groups formed or controlled by foreign stakeholders, cannot collect and preserve Chinese human genetic resources inside China or

---

[53] Financial Times. 2023. There is a new US national security obsession—Biotech. https://www.ft.com/content/cb9cd845-e9b0-4243-97f3-c315dac11fb4. Accessed on November 22, 2023.

[54] Reuters. 2023. US ads units China's BGI, Inspur to trade blacklist. www.reuters.com/markets/us/us-adds-chinese-genetics-company-units-trade-blacklist-2023-03-02/. Accessed on November 22, 2023.

[55] Financial Times. 2023. There is a new US national security obsession—Biotech. https://www.ft.com/content/cb9cd845-e9b0-4243-97f3-c315dac11fb4. Accessed on November 22, 2023.

[56] Biospace. 2019. Chinese CRISPR researcher receives 3-year prison sentence and $430,000 fine. www.biospace.com/article/china-jails-scientist-who-gene-edited-crispr-twins-/. Accessed on September 15, 2023.

take them outside of the country.[57] So this prohibits foreign companies from collecting human genetic resources inside China.

Given all this, it is thus possible that the biopharmaceutical industry could become a new focus area for strategic competition between the US and China. Investors are taking notice. 2023 saw global investors pulling back from China. In November of that year, it was reported that over 75% of foreign money—equal to US$25 billion—invested into Chinese stocks in 2023, had left the Chinese stock market.[58] Venture capitalists from the US and other countries have reduced investment in Chinese drug-makers. Not only does this reflect a global pullback in venture investment, it also highlights the perceived risks about China's economy and the rising geopolitical tensions. In the capital markets, the smart money has relocated from China to Singapore, while Western fund managers are under pressure from investors including global pension and sovereign funds to limit their exposure to China. In 2023 venture capital firm Sequoia Capital, one of the most famous global healthcare investors, and with a big China business, decided to separate into three independently run businesses: the US and European operations will retain the Sequoia name; the China outfit will be rebranded in English as HongChan. The India and Southeast Asia arms will be renamed Peak XV Partners.[59] The idea is to run the China business as a completely independent entity from its US operations. Pharmaceutical companies are contemplating the same scenario. A number of companies have carved already or are drawing up plans to carve out its China business as a way to shelter the company against mounting geopolitical tensions. In 2023 AstraZeneca, which is the UK's biggest listed company by market value at GB£ 183 billion, announced it was thinking about carving off its operations in China into a separate legal entity but would retain control of the business. The China part could then be listed again in Hong Kong and Shanghai which makes

---

[57] Genetic Literacy Project. 2022. China's new bioethics rules: Foreign companies prohibited from collecting human genetic resources inside China. https://geneticliteracyproject.org/2022/04/29/chinas-new-bioethics-rules-foreign-companies-prohibited-from-collecting-human-genetic-resources-inside-china/. Accessed on September 15, 2023.

[58] Financial Times. 2023. Over 75% of foreign money invested in Chinese stocks in 2023 has left. https://www.ft.com/content/20c5d5c8-dd64-4c22-a3fc-60d4a8336aeb. Accessed on November 22, 2023.

[59] Reuters. 2023. Private equity hurtles towards hard Asia reset. https://www.reuters.com/article/us-sequoia-restructuring-breakingviews-idDEKBN2XT06Y. Accessed on November 15, 2023.

it more of a domestic business. It would also tap a separate source of capital, mainly coming from China.[60]

The geopolitical tensions could also affect the regulatory space. As China's regulations are now aligned with international standards, Chinese drug development enters a new phase, changing innovative drug development from a single, local enterprise to simultaneous global registration. In the current geopolitical climate, it remains however to be seen whether China's transition to tighter regulations and global practices will be accepted by overseas regulators and other healthcare ecosystem stakeholders.[61] The risk therefore is that China's access to major markets will become much more limited. The FDA or EMEA might stop recognizing China-based trial data, in effect a return to pre-2017 conditions, when China wasn't part of the ICH and approvals in China required China-based trials. As a result of that, other countries might similarly decide not to recognize China-based trial data.[62] This then in turn could have severe consequences for venture capital. Investors might reduce investments in de Chinese biotech sector, and MNCs could scale down their China operations.

The problem is that all these protectionist measures in biotech will run against the core of what is a highly globalized, sector-spanning industry. The US and China currently share strong biotech ties both in R&D and commerce. China's bioeconomy sector has certainly benefited a great deal from many US tech and expertise transfers over the years. But the relationship between the two economic powerhouses has often worked both ways. This has particularly been clear in fundamental biotech research,

---

[60] Financial Times. 2023. AstraZeneca drafts plans to spin off China business amid tensions. www.ft.com/content/d195f3d0-0101-414e-b190-9691e6c5661d. Accessed on November 15, 2023.

[61] McKinsey & Co. 2022. Vision 2028: how China could impact the global biopharma industry. https://www.mckinsey.com/~/media/mckinsey/industries/life%20sciences/our%20insights/vision%202028%20how%20china%20could%20impact%20the%20global%20biopharma%20industry/vision-2028-how-china-could-impact-the-global-biopharma-industry.pdf. Accessed on November 19, 2023.

[62] McKinsey & Co. 2022. Vision 2028: how China could impact the global biopharma industry. https://www.mckinsey.com/~/media/mckinsey/industries/life%20sciences/our%20insights/vision%202028%20how%20china%20could%20impact%20the%20global%20biopharma%20industry/vision-2028-how-china-could-impact-the-global-biopharma-industry.pdf. Accessed on November 19, 2023.

where Chinese researchers have played a significant role in US biotechnology innovation through US-based R&D centers and incubators, as well as academic partnerships. Many US biopharma companies have been invested in by China-based funds. As such China was a source of capital for them, which was used to spur on innovation in the US. American life sciences companies also export a lot to China. The latter imports specialty and fine chemicals (including pharmaceutical ingredients) that so far is not produced at scale in the country. Another area that China relies on imports for, is lab equipment.

This all means that US, European and Chinese pharma companies need to rethink how they operate globally. Nobody can escape the geopolitical tensions, even if in the biotech space the perceived Chinese treat might be exaggerated. Fact is that in reality there are very few Chinese biotech firms with a global reach. Furthermore, across multiple sectors of the bioeconomy, the US is not only ahead of China on innovation, but also tops the global league. Therefore, the measures taken by the US are largely of a pre-emptive nature.[63] The US is thus not beating down the China biopharma sector but nipping its innovation in the bud. And while in the short run, the US biotechnology sector may benefit from protectionist measures, is questionable whether a scientific field so dependent on international collaboration will reap the same rewards.

BIOTECH MODEL 2.0

Because of these shortcomings of the past and the challenges ahead, a new kind of biotech company has emerged. Future Chinese biopharma companies will look a lot more like its US and European counterparts, with a core focus on own R&D, being less capital intensive, and having more in-depth capabilities. Therapies developed in-house will gradually become the pillar of Chinese drugmakers' pipelines as Chinese companies and investors become more sophisticated. Investors are now staying away from me-too assets or herding in certain therapeutic areas. They are looking at differentiation, more experienced management team and capabilities. Instead of the old overspending on multiple clinical programs that run simultaneously, now biotechs simply focus on primary disease indications

---

[63] World Bio Market Insights. 2022. The US-China tech war: Will biotech be next?. https://worldbiomarketinsights.com/the-us-china-tech-war-will-biotech-be-next/. Accessed on November 22, 2023.

and do not overspend on their R&D. Investors that remain in biotech investment will become more specialized and cautious, and are getting back to the basics, which are science and team. Chinese companies also start to be built from scratch as global companies with offices in different continents, instead of being a purely China-based company, as seen in the old model.

In other words, the new China biotech model looks very much like the US or European biotech model. But whatever the model, it's clear that any strategic partnership with a Chinese party could have a global potential. And despite the current global downturn, this model will be increasingly popular as it has a very clear potential for global expansion. When it comes to in-licensing, there is a greater focus on co-development with foreign companies, and making use of platform technologies, instead of in-licensing assets. Last but not least, Europe has moved to the foreground. As the China-US relations are deteriorating, many Chinese investors and biopharma companies are increasingly looking toward Europe for international partnerships (out-licensing, in-licensing and co-development).

China new biotech model 2.0

What	How	Why
Smaller financing rounds	Smaller A-Series and different value inflection points in smaller steps	Investors are more careful and want to reduce risk
In licensing of platform technologies	In license or co-develop first in class / best in class and early stage assets platform technologies	Global rights are more commercial valuable / platform technologies can create own IP
Smaller pipelines	Focus on a few core assets	Investors realize that an increased focus is required
Focus Europe	Europe is largely unexplored till now	Chinese biotechs increasingly realize that Europe is a world-class hub for early stage biotech technologies and assets
External service providers	Work more with CROs, CDMOS, etc	The less CAPEX investment, the better
China & global clinical trials	Outsourcing to globally active CROs	China remains an accelerator for technology validation, but global expansion is needed
Slower ROI	IPO or exits will take longer	Investors realize they need to adjust to the new normal

Source Agio Capital, Biopharma in China, a pivot to Europe. 2023

The Future Is Going Global

Despite all the geopolitical tensions, canceled partnerships, and regulatory hurdles, it is clear that a handful of China-originated biotechs have a strong global drive. The increasing number of out-licensing deals is a clear sign that Chinese innovation starts to go global. McKinsey notices that China-originated biopharma companies are also expanding globally. Looking at the top Chinese top biotechs, nine have established overseas footprints in numerous countries. Many have established R&D centers in the US, Europe and/or Australia, while some of them have built manufacturing sites in US and/or Europe. Some biotechs have strong enough pipelines from which some of their drugs have received, or are close to receiving, FDA approval. Such breakthroughs from China-originated biotechs are likeliest in the areas of oncology, small molecules, and antibodies. China's innovative drug developers are increasingly partnering with foreign companies to pitch their products overseas. Foreign pharma companies are also eager to leverage this wave of innovation. More and more US and European companies are thinking how to tap into China's assets, technology or innovation to create value ex-China.

As China is increasingly playing an important role in global drug competition and innovation, Western biopharma companies will face new challenges in their home markets. If Chinese biopharma succeeds in developing the same quality medicine, but at a much more affordable price, they can sell their drugs in foreign markets and compete head on with the competition abroad. This doesn't mean that Chinese drugmakers will set up large organizations abroad, like the Western MNCs. None of the China pharmaceutical or biopharma companies have enough launched products in their arsenal, nor a true global reach yet, let alone a sales force abroad. As we have seen the most promising way now for them to launch China-originated drugs abroad, is via international partnerships. This means that foreign companies should embrace a strategy of 'innovating with China', or 'in China for global'.

Despite all this, the internationalization of Chinese homegrown innovative drugs still has many hurdles to take. Whether all the me-too and me-better or even first-in-class drugs developed in China, will become accessible outside of the home market, remains an open question. Chinese drugmakers are clearly moving up the value chain but breaking into the most profitable markets of Europe and the US, will still remain a challenge for a lot of them. There is no clear path yet to realize the commercial potential of affordable innovation at scale outside of China. China-originated biopharmas are already pushing to get wider international distribution for products in this category, but experts do not expect affordable innovation from China to enter EU or US markets at scale by 2028.[64] These doubts reflect a perception about complex stakeholder dynamics -in particular, the expectation that powerful incumbents would create resistance. Chinese affordable innovation will catch on in selected markets and likely get a better reception in developing economies like Southeast Asia, the Middle East, Africa, and Latin America. These are all highly populous places where access to innovative drugs is still limited by cost and other factors. For these countries Chinese fast-follower or me-too and me-better therapies are an attractive proposition for local payers and patients. The distribution of affordable medications in these regions could be handled directly by the China-originated developer of the medications, but most likely a partnership with a multinational pharma company or a local player, is more feasible.[65] As we noticed ourselves over the last years, this is definitely a focus area for Chinese biopharmaceutical companies. When discussing regional licensing or technological partnerships with Western biotechs, the Chinese party increasingly asks for licensing rights for greater China and Southeast Asia. Chinese companies also increasingly focus on companies in Eastern Europe, which is also a more price-sensitive region.

But overall, despite all the challenges, there is enough reason to be confident about the long-term perspective of the Chinese biopharma sector and its global potential. Chinese biopharma companies are continuously evolving and upgrading, there is continued progress in regulatory integration with global standards, the level of early-stage investment is for now being sustained, and innovators are pivoting toward assets with global potential. The acquisition of Chinese CAR-T biotech Gracell at

---

[64] McKinsey & Co. 2022. Vision 2028: How China could impact the global biopharma industry. https://www.mckinsey.com/~/media/mckinsey/industries/life%20sciences/our%20insights/vision%202028%20how%20china%20could%20impact%20the%20global%20biopharma%20industry/vision-2028-how-china-could-impact-the-global-biopharma-industry.pdf. Accessed on November 19, 2023.

[65] McKinsey & Co. 2022. Vision 2028: How China could impact the global biopharma industry. https://www.mckinsey.com/~/media/mckinsey/industries/life%20sciences/our%20insights/vision%202028%20how%20china%20could%20impact%20the%20global%20biopharma%20industry/vision-2028-how-china-could-impact-the-global-biopharma-industry.pdf. Accessed on November 19, 2023.

the end of 2023 by AstraZeneca was also a new milestone, as partnerships between big biopharmas and China biotechs had so far been largely based on licensing/partnering, and not outright acquisition.[66] However, a big amount of M&A activity is unlikely to become a major exit path for China biopharma companies in the short and mid-term, as the quality of overall biotech portfolio is still an issue.

[66] Pharmaceutical Technology. 2023. AstraZeneca buys Chinese CAR-T biotech Gracell in a $1.2 bn deal. https://www.pharmaceutical-technology.com/news/astraz eneca-buys-chinese-car-t-biotech-gracell-in-a-1-2bn-deal/#:~:text=is%20transforming%20o ncology-,AstraZeneca%20buys%20Chinese%20CAR%2DT%20biotech%20Gracell%20in% 20a%20%241.2,to%20close%20in%20Q1%202024. Accessed on December 28, 2023.

Afterword

The growth and transformation story of the Chinese biopharma sector is unique. It's one of these feats which only China can pull off. In recent years, China has emerged as a global player in the biopharmaceutical industry, making significant strides in research, development and innovation. The country's commitment to fostering a robust biopharma sector is evident through substantial investments, collaborations and a growing pool of talented researchers. Despite the challenges in building a world class biopharma sector, China has been able to build a sector which is increasingly globally integrated. Driven by favorable regulatory reforms, the second biggest healthcare market, the need to get access to better medicines and healthcare facilities and government support, China has witnessed an unprecedented surge in biopharmaceutical investments, both from domestic and international sources. As a result, China has become a thriving hub for biopharma startups, research institutions and global pharmaceutical giants seeking collaboration opportunities.

China has become a major player in the production of biosimilars, generics and increasingly innovative medicines. The country's biopharma companies are focusing on developing high-quality, cost-effective innovative drugs, addressing the global demand for more accessible healthcare solutions. This trend is not only beneficial for the Chinese population but also contributes to the affordability of biopharmaceuticals on a global scale. Increasingly Chinese biopharma companies are also making significant contributions to global research and development efforts. Despite

© The Author(s), under exclusive license to Springer Nature Singapore Pte Ltd. 2024
S. Agten and B. Wu, *Biopharma in China*,
https://doi.org/10.1007/978-981-97-1471-1

their initial focus on me-too and me-better products, the emphasis on cutting-edge technologies, such as gene editing, RNA technologies and synthetic biology, is propelling China gradually to the forefront of scientific innovation. The country's research capabilities are increasingly being recognized, with a growing number of Chinese companies securing international patents and publications, and more and more collaboration with foreign research institutes, and out-licensing deals with western biopharma companies. Especially the latter proves to be a trend to be continued in the future and means that foreign companies are increasingly eying China to get access to cutting-edge technology. These partnerships facilitate knowledge exchange, joint research projects and the sharing of resources, contributing to a more interconnected and dynamic global biopharmaceutical landscape.

Despite the impressive advancements, the Chinese biopharmaceutical industry faces several challenges. China has seen its very first biopharma first boom and bust cycle which has left many companies and investors in distress. Other problems include the need for stringent regulatory frameworks, ensure product quality and safety and overcome concerns related to intellectual property protection. The Chinese government is actively addressing these issues, working toward establishing a regulatory environment that meets international standards. At the same time however, the government is also pursuing a policy of affordable innovation, where it tries to provide access to innovative but inexpensive medicines to the population. This is part of the 'Common prosperity' mantra. One of the by-results of this government push toward affordable innovation, is that it caps the commercial potential of biotechs. Investors therefore are becoming wary of investments in biotechs, as sales prices of drugs are increasingly controlled by the government. Furthermore, there are rising geopolitical tensions which hamper the internationalization of Chinese biopharma companies, which limits their access to lucrative foreign markets.

The future of biopharmaceuticals in China however still looks promising. Continued investments, a growing talent pool and a commitment to innovation, position China as a key player in shaping the future of healthcare. As the industry matures, we can expect to see even more groundbreaking therapies, advancements in personalized medicine and increased global collaborations that will contribute to addressing some of the world's most pressing healthcare challenges. China's biopharmaceutical industry has evolved rapidly, demonstrating a remarkable commitment to innovation and growth. The sector's success is attributed to strategic investments, improved research and a collaborative approach to addressing global healthcare needs. As China continues to shape the future of biopharma, the global market will see more innovative drugs from China. It is a certainty that more and more groundbreaking discoveries and advancements will emerge from this dynamic and thriving landscape.

Index

A
Abbvie, 119
Abogen, 80
Acquisition, 107, 108, 132, 133, 141, 142
Active Pharmaceutical Ingredients (API), 5, 6, 65, 134
Advantech Capital, 107
Affordable innovation, 74, 99, 126, 129, 141, 144
Africa, 118, 141
AI-driven drug discovery (AIDD), 84–86
America, 47, 118, 119, 134, 141
Amgen, 46
Antibody, 76, 77, 91, 119
Antibody drug conjugate (ADC), 76–78, 91, 93–95, 130
Antitrust Law, 24
Anti-Unfair Competition Law, 24
Apitope, 107
Apollomics, 56

Application, 24–28, 34, 35, 37, 38, 74, 75, 79, 83, 88, 117, 118, 125
Article, 82
Artificial Intelligence (AI), 37, 81, 83–85, 99
Asset, 51, 52, 54, 55, 65, 66, 74, 78, 79, 89–91, 94, 97–99, 105, 107, 108, 111, 116, 117, 119, 121, 131, 138–141
AstraZeneca (AZ), 11, 61, 88, 92, 129–131, 136, 142
AsymChem, 64
Australia, 89, 140
Autoimmune, 91, 107, 111

B
Backlog, 25, 38
Basic Medical Care and Health Promotion Law, 23
Bayer, 88
Beigene, 13, 46, 49, 55, 73, 75, 89, 98, 117–120, 128
Beijing, 14, 44, 54, 60, 83, 103, 125

© The Author(s), under exclusive license to Springer Nature Singapore Pte Ltd. 2024
S. Agten and B. Wu, *Biopharma in China*,
https://doi.org/10.1007/978-981-97-1471-1

147

Best-in-class, 52, 98
Biden, Joe, 133
Big Pharma, 49, 86–89, 117
Billion, 2, 4, 8–10, 13, 18, 28, 43, 44, 55, 56, 59, 64, 69, 84–86, 92, 93, 97, 103, 115, 119, 122, 131, 136
BioBAY, 61, 62, 72
BioEurope, 95
Biologics, 8, 13, 49, 55, 65, 75, 77, 94, 134
Biology, 86, 106, 144
Biomarker, 84
Biopharma, v, vi, 4, 6, 8, 12, 22, 24–27, 33, 34, 38, 42–44, 46, 48–50, 52, 53, 56, 58–60, 66, 68, 69, 72, 73, 76, 78, 81, 86, 89, 90, 92, 94, 98, 99, 105, 108, 111, 115, 119, 122, 126, 130, 138–140, 142, 143, 145
Biotech, vi, 8–10, 12, 33, 42, 45, 47, 50, 53–55, 59–61, 72, 92–94, 96, 106, 114–116, 121, 130, 132, 133, 137–139, 142
Biotechnology, 8, 54, 79, 133, 134, 138
Biotech park, vi, 60, 62, 72
Biotech Winter, 97, 115
Bispecific, 76, 77
Blockbuster, 89
Boao Lecheng International Medical Tourism Pilot Zone, 36
Boston Consulting Group, 60
Breakthrough, 82–84, 89–91, 96–98, 131, 132, 140
Breakthrough Therapy Designation (BTD), 12, 28, 42
Brii Biosciences, 44
Bristol Myers Squibb (BMS), 75, 120

C
Cancer, 17, 29, 73, 74, 77, 78, 90, 94, 95, 110, 118, 129
Cansino Biologics, 55
Capital, 42, 43, 50, 53–55, 58, 60, 80, 84, 88, 97, 102, 103, 105, 108, 115, 136, 138
Cardiovascular, 10, 16, 17, 67, 73, 128
CARsgen Therapeutics, 96
CAR-T, 79, 91, 95–97, 141
CBC Group, 102
Cell therapy, 72, 95, 96
Cellular Biomedicine Group, 79
Center of Drug Evaluation (CDE), 27, 37–39
Central nervous system (CNS), 10, 67
Chapter 18AA, 54, 56
Chemical, 8, 34, 127, 138
Chemistry, 65, 81, 86, 106
Chengdu, 60, 87
China, v, vi, 2–8, 10–19, 22–31, 33–39, 44–46, 48, 50–52, 54, 55, 57, 58, 63–66, 68, 73–75, 78–80, 82, 84–86, 89, 92, 93, 95–98, 102, 103, 105, 107, 109–111, 116–118, 122, 123, 125, 126, 128, 130–133, 135, 136, 138, 140, 143–145
China angle, 102, 109
ChinaBio, 43
China Food and Drug Administration (CFDA), 23
China for China' strategy@'China for China' strategy, 73, 87
China Healthcare Summit, 68, 114, 116
China National Intellectual Property Administration (CNIPA), 34, 35
Chinese Communist party (CCP), 124
Chronic, 127

INDEX

circRNA, 80
Citizen, 2, 13, 16, 18, 19, 23, 25, 29, 122
Clinical, 7, 28, 31, 51, 73, 75, 108, 117, 131, 138
Clinical trials, 12, 26, 27, 33, 36, 42, 47, 51, 54, 65–67, 77, 78, 84, 85, 87, 89, 94–96, 105, 117, 118, 120
Combo therapies, 76
Commercial, 12, 19, 24, 48, 73, 97, 126, 133, 141, 144
Committee on Foreign Investment in the United States (CFIUS), 133
Common prosperity, 122, 124, 144
Companies, v, vi, 4–8, 10–12, 26, 30–34, 36, 38, 43, 44, 46–49, 51–56, 59, 61, 62, 64, 68, 72–75, 77, 79, 80, 88, 89, 92, 93, 95–97, 102, 103, 106, 115, 120, 126, 130, 132, 134, 138, 140, 141, 144
Compound, 19, 74, 95
Conditional Approval (CA), 28
Consumer, 10, 17, 18, 69
Consumption, 16, 18
Contract and Development Manufacturing Organization (CDMO), 33, 61, 63–65, 117
Contract Research Organization (CRO), 64
Covid, 6, 111, 115, 122–124
CRISPR, 78, 135
CSI medical services index, 125
CStone Pharmaceuticals, 44, 46, 49, 52, 77, 116

D

Department of Commerce, 133
De-risking, 133
Development, vi, 8, 11, 12, 19, 22, 23, 25, 28, 33, 37, 38, 42, 47, 51, 59–61, 63, 66, 74, 77, 78, 81, 86, 87, 93, 96, 105, 106, 108, 111, 117, 130, 133, 139, 143
Diabetes, 16, 110, 111, 122, 127, 128
Diagnosis, 23, 34, 80, 84
Disease, 2, 5, 16, 23, 28, 34, 67, 73, 74, 95, 107, 110–112, 127, 128, 138
dMed, 65
DNA, 106, 135
Doctor, 14, 15, 84, 124, 125
Doctorate, 81
Domestic, 2, 4, 11, 42, 55, 59, 63, 73–75, 84, 129, 130, 132, 133, 143
Drug, v, 2–8, 11, 12, 25–27, 29–33, 36, 38, 47, 51, 52, 72, 73, 75–77, 81, 85, 89, 90, 114, 117–119, 124, 127, 131, 143, 145
Drug Administration Law, 23
Drug makers, 7, 8, 29, 128
Duality Biologics, 94

E

Eccogene, 92
Economical, 133
Economy, v, vi, 2, 3, 14, 84, 122, 136
Ecosystem, v, 51, 60–62, 64, 66, 68, 73, 85, 86, 88, 97, 99, 108, 114, 117, 137
Eight Roads, 102
EMEA, 27, 65, 97, 118, 137
Engineering, 76, 99
Entity List, 135
Entrepreneur, 49, 106
Equipment, 4, 18, 23, 125, 138
Erasmus University, 107
eTheRNA, 108

Europe, vi, 6, 24, 26, 27, 35, 47, 50, 53, 59, 60, 63, 75, 78, 83, 87, 98, 104, 106, 109, 115, 139, 141
Everest Medicines, 52
Executive, vi, 12, 47, 49, 98, 105, 133
Expenditure, 18, 115, 123, 124

F
Fast follower, vi, 73, 74, 76
FDA, 27, 37–39, 65, 78, 90, 95, 97, 117, 118, 140
Fidelity, 102
Financial, 55, 59, 102, 105, 109, 111, 119, 121, 122, 130, 133
First-in-class, 52, 72–74, 79, 115, 128, 131, 140
Forbion, 45
Foreign, vi, 4, 11, 12, 25, 27, 33, 34, 38, 46, 95, 105, 107, 108, 110, 130–132, 135, 140, 144
Foreign Direct Investment (FDI), 102, 132
Fosun Kite Biotechnology, 79
Fosun Pharma, 11, 79, 105
France, 44, 60
Full-Life Technologies, 80
Fund, vi, 18, 43, 45, 51, 68, 102, 103, 109, 136, 138

G
GDP, 2, 3, 68, 122
Gene and cell editing, 78
Gene and cell therapy (GCT), 95
Genentech, 74
General Practitioner (GP), 15
Generic drugs, 7, 8, 32, 72, 123, 129
Generics, 4, 6, 7, 25, 26, 65, 143
Gene therapy, 72, 79, 81
Genetic, 110, 135

Genor Biopharma, 44
Geopolitical, 6, 48, 134, 136, 137, 140, 144
Germany, 18, 44
Gilead Sciences, 79
Global, v, 2, 6, 10, 11, 17, 18, 26, 27, 44–46, 52, 64, 65, 69, 74, 76, 81, 83, 85, 87, 89, 90, 94, 96–98, 103, 104, 108, 115, 120, 126, 133, 136, 138, 140, 145
GLP-1, 78, 92, 116
Golden Age, 42
Government, 2, 6, 8, 11, 18, 22, 24, 28, 30, 32, 48, 60, 105, 114, 121–124, 126, 132, 134, 144
Gracell, 141
Grand Pharma, 11, 105, 108
Greater Bay Area, 37, 60
Growth, v, vi, 2, 3, 8–10, 12, 16, 19, 42, 51, 53, 58, 60, 69, 83, 92, 93, 95, 110, 114, 115, 122, 145
GSK, 49, 94, 124
Guangzhou, 14, 60
Guangzhou Bio-Island, 61
Guideline, 23, 26, 27, 37, 39, 135

H
Hainan, 36, 37
Hangzhou, 54, 60
Hansoh Pharma, 94, 105
Harbour Biomed, 49, 77, 107
Harvard, 104
Healthcare, v, 2, 3, 8, 13–16, 18, 29, 36, 42–45, 49, 59, 73, 83, 102, 131, 143–145
Health technology assessment (HTA), 123
Healthy China 2030, v, 2, 22, 23, 25
He, Jiankui, 135
Hengrui, 11, 75, 95, 98, 105, 128
Hillhouse Capital, 102, 108
Hinova, 80

INDEX 151

Homegrown, v, 22, 65, 75, 95, 97, 140
Hong Kong, 52, 54, 59, 114, 120, 136
Hong Kong Science and Technology Parks (HKSTP), 88
Hong Kong Stock Exchange (HKEX), 12, 42, 53–56, 59, 60
Hospital, 13, 15, 32, 73, 106, 110, 124, 131
Hua Medicine, 49, 73
Hutchison, 73

I
IASO Biotherapeutics, 96
I-Campus, 88
IDG Capital, 45
I-Mab Biopharma, 49, 77
'in China for global' strategy, 90, 140
Incubation, 61, 88, 89, 106–108
Industry, vi, 2–4, 9, 10, 16, 22, 37, 49, 53, 60, 62, 64, 66, 67, 76, 79, 81, 83, 84, 86, 95, 97, 103, 115, 116, 124, 130, 132, 137, 144
Infectious, 28, 67, 111, 112
Inhibitor, 74, 116, 117, 119, 129, 130
In-license, 51, 52, 93, 105, 106, 111
InnoCare Pharma, 55
Innovation, v, vi, 22, 25, 33, 49, 50, 55, 57, 58, 60, 61, 66, 68, 72–74, 76, 83, 86, 88–90, 95, 97–99, 105, 106, 116, 130, 138, 140, 143, 145
Innovator, vi, 7, 26, 35, 36, 98, 141
Innovent Biologics, 13, 49, 73–75
Insilico Medicine, 85
Institution, 13–15, 23, 24, 26, 29, 32, 33, 117, 125, 135, 143
Insurance, 3, 13, 18, 19, 23, 123, 126

Intellectual Property (IP), 48, 144
International, 15, 22, 24, 26, 27, 39, 49, 60, 64, 79, 82, 88, 96, 97, 105, 106, 120, 137–140
International Conference on Harmonization of Technical Requirements for Registration of Pharmaceuticals for Human Use (ICH), 25
Investigational New Drug Application (IND), 68
Investment, v, vi, 4, 42–44, 46, 64, 83, 103, 106, 115, 121, 132, 133, 139, 144
IPO, 54, 56, 57, 59, 108, 115, 116, 120, 121, 125

J
Jacobio Pharmaceuticals, 119
Japan, vi, 5, 27, 28, 63, 87, 119
Jing-Jin-Ji area, 60
Jointown Pharmaceutical Group, 11
Journal, 82
Jumpcan Pharmaceuticals, 11
Juno Therapeutics, 79
Junshi Biosciences, 49, 55, 73, 75, 118
JW Therapeutics, 79, 96, 128

K
Kelun, 94
Kite Pharma, 79

L
Lanova Medicines, 94
Law, 6, 23, 33, 34
Legal, 22, 23, 134, 136
Legend Biotech, 79, 96
Lighthouse Capital, 45
Lily Asia Ventures, 45

LNP delivery, 111
Lyfe Capital, 102
Lynk Pharmaceuticals, 80

M
Management, 48, 103, 116, 138
Manufacturing, 2, 4, 7, 8, 12, 26, 33, 49, 79, 133, 134, 140
Market, v, 2, 3, 6, 8, 9, 11, 16, 22, 24, 26, 28, 32, 35, 38, 49, 53, 55, 56, 59, 63, 69, 74, 85, 97, 102, 108, 110, 115, 116, 120, 126, 130, 137, 140, 145
Marketing Authorization (MA), 35
Marketing Authorization Holder (MAH), 26, 32
McKinsey, 43, 57, 58, 66, 68, 69, 76, 78, 81, 86, 91, 98, 114–116
Me-better, 73, 74, 110, 140, 141, 144
Mechanism of Action (MoA), 52, 73, 77, 79, 80, 116
Medical, 2, 13–15, 18, 19, 23, 37, 83, 84, 125, 132
Medicines, v, 2, 7, 11, 12, 22, 25, 29, 38, 47, 51, 52, 74, 98, 105, 125, 126, 132, 144
Medtech, 59, 131, 132
Meheco, 11
Melanoma, 110
Merck, 46, 49, 75, 94, 129
Metabolic, 10, 67, 73, 108
METiS Therapeutics, 80
Me-too, 72–74, 98, 110, 138, 140, 141, 144
Middle class, 8, 18, 110
Military, 135
Million, 9, 13, 14, 16, 17, 32, 43, 45, 48, 80, 92, 94, 98, 107, 112, 119, 124, 130
Ministry of Science and Technology (MOST), 62
MIT, 104
Model, 50, 51, 61, 85, 89, 108, 116, 131, 139
Molecule, 51, 65, 72–75, 85, 88, 90, 140
Mortality, 17
mRNA, 72, 80, 81, 108
MSCI China Health Care Index, 58
MSD, 11, 120
Multinational (MNC), 64, 72, 75, 88, 89, 91, 103, 120, 128, 130, 140
Multiple sclerosis (MS), 111

N
Nanfung Life Sciences, 102, 108
NASDAQ, 53, 55, 56, 108
National Biotechnology and Biomanufacturing Initiative (NBBI), 134
National Essential Drug List (NEDL), 29
National Healthcare Security Administration (NHSA), 22–24, 31
National Health Commission of China, 125
National Medical Products Administration (NMPA), 12, 22–28, 36, 37, 42, 50, 75, 76, 87, 95, 105
National Reimbursement Drug List (NRDL), 12, 24, 26, 28–31, 42, 52, 74, 123, 126–131
Nature, 77, 81, 82, 138
NDA (New Drug Application), 25, 28, 96, 97
Next-generation, 18
Novartis, 11, 61, 91, 119, 120, 130
Novel, 12, 42, 76–79, 83, 95, 108, 111
Novo Holdings, 45
Nuclear-acid, 72

Nurse, 14

O
Obesity, 16
Oncology, 8, 25, 31, 46, 67, 73, 76, 77, 88, 91, 118, 119, 128, 140
Orbimed, 102, 103, 108
Orphan drug, 127
Out-license, 52, 94, 120
Over the counter (OTC), 6, 7

P
Pandemic, 6, 18, 79, 80, 111, 115, 122, 124, 134
Patent, 6, 7, 26, 33–35, 83, 88, 127, 129
Patent Law, 26, 33–35
Patent Term Extension (PTE), 35
Patient, 30, 36, 83, 84, 117, 130
PD-1/PD-L1 inhibitor, 74, 116, 129, 130
PD-1 inhibitor, 74, 117, 119, 120
People, 2, 13–16, 28, 47, 48, 74, 110, 125, 131
People's Republic of China (PRC), 3
Pfizer, 46, 61, 93, 129, 130
Pharmaceutical, v, 3–6, 10–12, 22, 26, 30, 31, 35, 38, 47, 61, 83, 87, 88, 103, 106, 115, 124, 126, 133, 140, 144
Pharmaron, 64
Phase I, 66
Phase II, 54, 66, 94, 96
Phase III, 66
PhD, 81
Pipeline, 51, 52, 73, 74, 89, 106–108, 121, 138, 140
PMDA, 27
Policy, 11, 15, 25, 26, 30, 32, 42, 102, 105, 122–124, 126, 131–133, 144

Political, 133
Population, v, 2, 3, 8, 12, 15, 18, 19, 73, 78, 110, 111, 117, 122, 143, 144
Premium, 11, 19, 29, 32
Price, 8, 23, 24, 26, 28, 30–32, 114, 123, 125, 127, 129, 141, 144
Price negotiation, 30, 31
Priority Review (PR), 27, 28
Priority Review System, 25, 27, 28
Private, 4, 13, 83, 124, 126
Private Equity (PE), 103, 136
Procurement, 4, 26, 32, 123, 131
Production, 5, 6, 26, 33, 105, 106, 132, 134, 143
Products, 2, 8, 11, 12, 18, 22, 26, 28, 31, 37, 42, 52, 95, 98, 110, 127, 129, 131, 141, 144
Profit, 12, 33, 42, 68, 79, 114
Proprietary technology, 33, 51, 107
PROTAC, 80
Protectionist, 131, 137
Protein, 76, 111
Protocol, 27, 36
Public, 11, 13, 23, 28–30, 32, 53, 56, 58, 122, 124, 132
Publication, 81, 82, 144

Q
Qiming Ventures, 45, 103
Quality, v, 2, 7, 8, 11, 18, 22, 28, 33, 36, 49, 52, 64, 65, 82, 106, 116, 120, 126, 140, 142–144
Quan Capital, 102

R
Radiopharmaceuticals, 80, 81, 111
Rare disease, 25, 28, 37, 126–128
Raw materials, 4, 6
Real-world evidence (RWE), 36

Reforms, v, 2, 8, 11, 24, 25, 32, 38, 42, 50, 53, 56, 124, 143
Reformulation, 34
Registration, 15, 25–27, 74, 97, 137
Regulations, 6, 23, 38, 39, 56, 122, 135, 137
Regulatory, 8, 11, 23–28, 35–37, 39, 42, 54, 98, 117, 137, 143, 144
Reimbursement, 18, 19, 24, 28, 31, 123
RemeGen, 55, 93, 130
Research and Development (R&D), 8, 23, 26, 33, 50, 51, 53, 60, 72, 73, 80, 83, 84, 87–89, 97, 108, 115, 121, 133, 137, 139, 140, 143
Returnee, 49, 50, 114
Review, 12, 25–27, 39, 133
Ribo Life Sciences, 80
RMB, 9, 102, 103
RNA, 80, 111, 144
RNAi, 91, 92, 108
Roche, 11, 61, 87, 120, 129
Rona Therapeutics, 80
Rural, 3, 19

S

Sales, 8, 11, 12, 87, 97, 105, 106, 121, 124, 125, 130, 131, 140, 144
Sanofi, 11, 49, 85, 87
SA (Special Approval), 28
Science, 48, 60, 84, 88, 139
Scientist(s), 12, 47, 48, 50, 72, 82, 97
SCPC Pharmaceutical, 11
Sea turtle, 47, 48, 50
Securities Regulatory Commission (CSRC), 120, 121
Sequence, 121
Sequoia Capital, 102, 136

Shanghai, vi, 14, 44, 54, 55, 60, 62, 87, 107, 108, 136
Shanghai Pharmaceuticals, 11, 88
Shanghai Stock Exchange's Science and Technology Innovative Board (STAR), 12, 42, 53, 55, 56
Shenzhen, 55, 60, 108, 125
Silicon Valley, 17, 44–46, 104
Singapore, 136
Sinopharm, 11
Sinotau, 80
siRNA, 72
Smoker, 17
Social Security Law, 23
Society, 15, 16
Soffinova, 45
South America, 118
South Korea, 18
Special Purpose Acquisition Companies (SPAC), 56
Startup, 43, 44, 49, 50, 53, 119, 143
State Administration of Market Regulation (SAMR), 22–24
STEM, 81
Stemirna, 80
Strategy, 73–75, 79, 87, 89, 120, 126, 134
Supplementary Protection Certificates (SPCs), 35
Supply chain, 6, 11, 125, 134
Suzhou, 54, 60–62, 72, 103
Synthetic, 144
System, 13, 17, 18, 22, 23, 26–28, 30, 33, 35, 39, 122, 124

T

Takeda, 129
Talent, 47–50, 61, 62, 86, 97, 144
Technological, 62, 133, 141
Technology, 2, 3, 47, 48, 55, 77, 90, 106, 107, 116, 123, 132, 133, 144

Therapy, 42, 77, 80, 95
Thousands Talents Plan, 48
Traditional Chinese Medicine (TCM), 7
Treatment, 7, 9, 15, 23, 25, 28, 29, 34, 77, 78, 95, 96, 126

U
United Nations, 16
United States (US), vi, 4, 6, 7, 28, 35, 48, 49, 51, 56, 59, 63, 78, 82, 89, 109, 111, 118, 133, 134, 138, 140, 141
University, 61
Urban, 3, 15, 18
USD, 102

V
Venture Capital (VC), 42, 43, 58, 60, 80, 84, 105, 115, 136, 137
Vivo Capital, 102, 103, 108
Volume Based Procurement (VBP), 26, 32

W
Western, 4–7, 48, 61, 80, 90, 98, 109, 111, 127, 128, 130, 136, 144
Worg Pharmaceuticals, 107
World, v, vi, 2, 3, 17, 43, 50, 63, 64, 77, 81, 89, 95, 98, 110, 112, 123, 134, 144
Wuhan, 14, 61
Wuxi, 60
Wuxi AppTec, 13, 64, 79
WuXi Biologics, 65, 134

X
Xi, Jinping, 124
XtalPi, 85

Y
Yangtze River Delta, 60
YS Biopharma, 56

Z
Zai Lab, 49, 52, 75, 77, 102
Zhangjiang High-Tech Park, vi, 61, 62

Printed in the United States
by Baker & Taylor Publisher Services